DATE DUE

DEC 1 1 2001		
APR 0 8 2003		
APR 1 8 2003		

A FINE WILL BE CHARGED FOR EACH
OVERDUE MATERIAL.

THE SOCIAL ORGANIZATION
OF THE MODERN PRISON

THE SOCIAL ORGANIZATION OF THE MODERN PRISON

Aida Y. Hasaballa

Criminology Studies
Volume 14

The Edwin Mellen Press
Lewiston•Queenston•Lampeter

Library of Congress Cataloging-in-Publication Data

Hasaballa, Aida Y.
   The social organization of the modern prison / Aida Y. Hasaballa.
      p. cm. -- (Criminology studies ; v. 14)
   Includes bibliographical references and index.
   ISBN 0-7734-7616-4
   1. Prisons--United States. 2. Prisons--Washington (D.C.) 3. Organizational sociology.
   4. Lorton Correctional Complex (Washington, D.C.) I. Title. II. Series.

   HV9471 .H37   2001
   365'.973--dc21

                                           00-060921

| This is volume 14 in the continuing series |
| Criminology Studies |
| Volume 14 ISBN 0-7734-7616-4 |
| CrS Series ISBN 0-7734-8583-X |

A CIP catalog record for this book is available from the British Library.

The Edwin Mellen Press
Box 450
Lewiston, New York
USA 14092-0450

The Edwin Mellen Press
Box 67
Queenston, Ontario
CANADA L0S 1L0

The Edwin Mellen Press, Ltd.
Lampeter, Ceredigion, Wales
UNITED KINGDOM SA48 8LT

Printed in the United States of America

To my loving parents, for giving me life...
and my husband and daughter for helping me live it

Table of Contents

List of Illustrations

Preface

Let us suppose that there is a widespread epidemic of a dangerous disease that has been plaguing our country for the past hundred years. The "cure" for this disease has been used since its inception in various amounts, forms and doses. Unfortunately, the alleged cure has, over the years, been found to not only fail to cure the problem but in many cases even exacerbate the symptoms. Would society stand for this obvious detriment to the integrity of scientific inquiry and research? This disease I am referring to is criminal behavior and the cure is the American penal system. The number of individuals incarcerated in the U.S. is unmatched anywhere else in the modern industrialized world. More importantly this trend is increasing at an astonishing rate. Ironically, this trend is not matched by the subsequent decline in criminality by individuals of all social classes. As citizens of a democratic society, it is our duty and obligation to make sure that social policies reflect an accurate representation of the investment we make in prisons.

This book began as a research inquiry into the modern prison system, with a focus on the various dilemmas associated with the problem of crime and punishment. It epitomizes the scientific methodology of field research, with its ethnographic focus on providing the reader with a penetrating and insightful look at prison life in the modern penal institution. Society has a rough idea of what might go on inside the walls of a prison. Unfortunately, this image is often presented in a manner which neglects, misrepresents and even distorts the true dynamics of prison organization. It is only through the careful observation of the routine operation of a prison institution and the daily interaction with those living in captivity, can we begin to understand the true meaning of incarceration for the offender and for the community as a whole. This work is a revealing look at prison life from the inside out. It provide us with a glimpse of reality from the perspective of the offender and also gives a first hand glimpse of the turmoil, and dilemmas faced by correctional staff. We are allowed the unique opportunity to reap the benefits of a comprehensive qualitative task, as the author has combined the various techniques of observation, interview, participant-observation, oral history and field experiment, to provide us with a captivating and scientific understanding of the various organizational

i

elements of the modern prison, which updates the literature on prison social organization.

Journey Behind Bars brings to light the most urgent and pressing issues related to prison policies today. It addresses the recent rise in prison populations and the associated problems of over-crowding, gang violence, drug trafficking and increase in youth offenders, as a testimony to the fact that state and federal correctional systems are far from adequate. The author attempts to explain the various reasons for these facts and to arrive at a comprehensive understanding of the various structural elements and organizational dynamics of the system of corrections that may be contributing to the problem. This book will enrich the reader's understanding of why there is an increasingly violent and uncontrollable population of incarcerated individuals emerging, along with a system of growing tolerance by staff for rule violation. We can finally focus on the long term trend that is heading toward the creation of a class of criminals who are caught up in a cycle of criminal activity, referred to by many individuals as the "revolving door" of prisons. There is a realistic and bold attempt by the author to surface the often neglected question of "why"? Why do our criminal justice policies seem to lay the foundations of failure and handicap efforts that may truly have a positive impact on criminality. These difficult questions are addressed towards the end through an in-depth analysis of the data, which lends empirical credibility to the theoretical ideology of Conflict Criminology.

Aida Hasaballa has, through this text, provided us with the unique synthesis between descriptive ethnology and the urgent need to address those critical issues related to crime and punishment that are often jaded by political rhetoric. It is hoped that this book will help stimulate the ongoing debate over prisons towards a practical approach which bridges the gap between the administrative legislation of penal policy and the realistic outcomes of their implementation on both inmates and correctional staff. Regardless of your views on prisons and prison reform, this text will undoubtedly commit the reader to search for solutions which serve our ultimate goal of rehabilitative correction.

Dr. William J. Chambliss
Professor of Criminal Justice
George Washington University

Acknowledgments

Where do I begin? This work was undoubtedly a labor of love on the part of many people who collectively inspired, encouraged, patiently persevered and actively participated in the final outcome of this project. I want to thank Dr. William Chambliss for his countless efforts in helping me advance my research and career. He was truly the definitional epitome of a mentor and friend. I merely hope that this work can only capture my endless pursuit of excellence in research that has been my example in Dr. Chambliss.

And of course, Mrs. Anne Knight...the true example of love and sacrifice. A lady who had dedicated a lifetime to volunteering to work inside the walls of a prison to educate and motivate those individuals who have been rejected by society. Without the efforts of Mrs. Knight in helping me gain access to the facility, setting up meetings and interviews, connecting me with the right people, teaching me how to do research inside a prison, none of this would have been even remotely feasible.

Then there are those long laborious hours of endless frustrations, confusions, mis-haps, and "I can't take this anymore". Who can put up with the publication of a manuscript other than a loving and supporting family. Files erased, data missing, deadlines to meet, discs destroyed, and that god-awful task of deciphering my own handwriting — I've just about went through it all. And there was my husband, right along with me, putting the pieces back together and my parents, helping me maintain my sanity. A special thanks to them for this true labor of love.

iii

CHAPTER ONE: INTRODUCTION

After a period of considerable popularity in the 1950s, sociological research on prisons experienced a period of dormancy. The groundbreaking works of Clemmer, Sykes, Cressey, Irwin and others have been the primary source of information about the social organization and culture of prisons. In the 1960s and 1970s, research and theory on prisons shifted to a concern over the role of imprisonment in the larger socio-political economic structure, as manifested in the works of Rusche and Kirchheimer, Reasons, Wilkins, Reiman and others.

Recently, a few studies of prisons as a social environment have re-appeared in the works of Colvin, Jacobs, Marquart, Sampson and Laub and Davidson. The purpose of their research is to assess the degree to which the prison as a social organization has changed to accommodate the shifts in socio-political economic structure, which has a direct impact on the structure of imprisonment. There are two fundamental issues facing contemporary American society that are affecting the criminal justice system (Bales and Dees, 1992). The first of these is the growing surplus population composed of those individuals who are either not needed by or cannot be accommodated in the system of economic production. These individuals include the uneducated, unemployed, under-employed, the poor, street criminals, and deviants of all sorts and ages. The organization and operation of the economic structure in American society is marginalizing these people and likewise increasing their potential for criminal activity. At the same time, there is a push toward the expansion of the various mechanisms of social control, including the criminal justice system.

However, this demand is complicated by the second societal problem, which is that at the very time the criminal justice system is asked to expand and be more effective, the means to finance such proposals are receding due to the fiscal crisis faced by local, state and federal governments. This apparent structural contradiction has led to the ineffective control of individuals dedicated to a life of law-violating behavior (Bales and Dees, 1992; Tonry, 1993). Accordingly, important trends in the ideological basis of penal policies have culminated into an unprecedented growth in prison populations (Tonry, 1993). From 1977 to 1982, 37 states passed mandatory sentencing laws and 11 states passed determinate sentencing laws (Tonry, 1993). The advent of the U.S. Sentencing Commission's guidelines in November of 1987 also brought about significant changes. Under the federal guidelines, offenders are less likely to receive probation and more likely to receive a mandatory minimum prison term (Saltzburg, 1993). Moreover, under the Federal Sentencing Guidelines parole is abolished, therefore compounding the problem of over-crowding by eliminating the possibility of release upon showing an inmate's good conduct and institutional adjustment (Tonry, 1993; Saltzburg, 1993).

Moreover, in 1984, Congress passed the Comprehensive Crime Control Act which called for the use of strict sentencing guidelines - the Federal Sentencing Guidelines - by judges in the Federal system. The Act was designed to (1) produce comprehensiveness and consistency in Federal law sentencing; (2) assure fairness in sentencing procedures; (3) create a certainty in an offender's release date; (4) provide an availability in sentencing options; and (5) assure that the Federal criminal justice system will adhere to a consistent sentencing philosophy (U.S. Code of Congressional and Administrative News, 1984: 3233-3242). Thus, the bill was an attempt by Congress to require the Sentencing Commission to recommend changes in current sentencing practices to make punishment more suitable to the specific needs and characteristics of each offender. However, critics note that the Sentencing Guidelines simply shifts discretion from the sentencing judge to the prosecutor, and debates continue as to

2

whether or not disparities in sentencing have actually been reduced (Saltzburg, 1993). There is a growing concern over the exercise of discretion by prosecutors who use the plea bargaining process to circumvent the sentence recommended by the sentencing guidelines, if he does not agree with the recommendation. These sentencing practices have had the net effect of creating a significant population of long-term prison inmates and has produced what is known today in the criminological and popular literatures as a "crisis" in criminal justice (Bales and Dees, 1992). One effect of such policies and practices has been to increase problems of control and management within the prison (Feeley and Simon, 1992). Thus, a central feature of the emerging penal practices is to shift from a focus on punishment or rehabilitation to "identifying and managing unruly groups...it is concerned with the rationality of managerial processes and [its] goal is not to eliminate crime but to make it tolerable through systematic coordination" (Feeley and Simon, 1992). Thus, the impact of current penal ideology is to further divert attention away from the particular needs of the individual offender. There is an increasing focus on the aggregation of groups of offenders according to the "degree of control warranted by their risk profiles," (Feeley and Simon, 1992), masking the significant differences in cases amongst offenses and offenders.

These dynamics have culminated in an epidemic of violence behind prison walls (Colvin, 1992). Gang activities have come to shape the structure of interaction amongst prisoners and staff (Irwin, 1980; Jacobs, 1983; Fong and Buentello, 1991). Gangs increasingly are formed through social networks made in free society, that are carried into the prison. Moreover, these gangs tend to be dominated by cliques of young men who purposely violate the old convict code, when for decades, notes Irwin, the "potentially obstreperous and conflictive population was held in a tentative peace by prisoner leaders, a code, and the constant threat of extreme force" (Irwin, 1980: 212). Prison gangs come to hate and distrust each other and are increasingly antagonistic to the administration. The emergence of prison gangs also has come to control and expand the inmate

3

contraband system, especially the trafficking and distribution of drugs (Colvin, 1992: 211). There is thus significant reason to believe that prisons have undergone substantial change in the structure of their social organization. The most profound change in prison populations has been the increase in the number of inmates incarcerated in State and Federal institutions (U.S. Department of Justice, Bureau of Justice Statistics: 1993). The total population of State and Federal inmates increased from 329,821 in 1980 to 948,881 in 1993 (see table 1). The rapid growth in prison populations has compounded the problem of overcrowding (Feeley and Simon, 1992). One strategy employed by prison officials is to house new prisoners in jail temporarily until a space becomes available in the prison. However, this is becoming increasingly difficult as conditions of overcrowding in jails are almost as rampant as those in prisons (Mitchell, 1994). Another strategy employed by State and Federal institutions to cope with overcrowding is to double-bunk inmates in cells, rooms or cubicles designed for only one person (Saltzburg, 1993). The American Correctional Association has set the minimum size for an individual's prison cell at 60 square feet, however, because of overcrowding, only about one fifth of U.S. inmates have cells that meet this standard (Saltzburg, 1993). Living standards under such conditions have enhanced the climate of pressure and anxiety within the prison (Saltzburg, 1993). With personal space limited and goods and resource scarce, tensions rise, suspicions mount and explosive acts of violence become commonplace acts of force and aggression (Fong and Buentello, 1991).

Moreover, the dynamics of sentencing policies and procedures, along with the criminal justice system's bias towards certain types of crimes and certain kinds of offenders have resulted in a disproportionate amount of inmates who are young, male, black, poor and under- educated, as it is this group of individuals who are most likely to commit the street crimes that are most represented in crime statistics (U.S. Department of Justice, Bureau of Justice Statistics: 1993). Whereas White inmates comprise 43% of the prisoners and 83.3% of the total population, African American inmates comprise 37.3% of the prisoners and 12.4% of the total population (see table 2). Also, in 1991, 65% of State prisoners had not completed high school (Beck et al., 1993). Furthermore, the highest rate of incarceration occurs between the ages of 20 and 29; between 1980 and 1991, the incarceration rate of both white and black males in that age group more than doubled, producing a significant population of young, poorly educated, incorrigible, unmanageable youthful offenders who are intolerant to authority (U.S. Department of Justice, Bureau of Justice Statistics: 1993). Another significant change in the composition of prisons today is a result of the increase in frequency and length of sentences for drug offenses. New court commitments to State prisons increased for drug offenses from a little over 10.0% in 1980 to almost 40.0% in 1990 (U.S. Department of Justice, Bureau of Justice Statistics: 1993). Moreover, inmates are more frequently involved in drug use before entering prison and thus they continue to support their habit once incarcerated (U.S. Department of Justice, Bureau of Justice Statistics: 1991). In 1991, about 80% of inmates reported using some type of drug at sometime of their life and 25% reported using cocaine or crack in the month before the offense for which they were currently incarcerated. Thus, prisons and especially prison economics have increasingly become an opportunity for the expansion of the drug market with its associated problems of disputes, violence and retaliation (Fleisher, 1989; Sampson and Laub, 1993; Pontell and Welsh, 1994). The following tables summarize significant changes in prisons and prison populations between1980 and 1993:

Table 1. Change in State and Federal Prison Populations 1980–1993

Year	Number of Inmates	Annual Percent Change	Total Percent Change Since 1980
1980	329,821	——	——
1981	369,930	12.2 %	12.2 %
1882	413,806	11.9	25.5
1983	436,855	5.6	32.5
1984	462,002	5.8	40.1
1985	502,507	8.8	52.4
1986	544,972	8.5	65.2
1987	585,084	7.4	77.4
1988	627,600	7.3	90.3
1989	712,364	13.5	116.0
1990	773,919	8.6	134.6
1991	825,619	6.7	150.3
1992	883,656	7.0	167.9
1993	948,881	7.4	187.7

Source: "Prisoners in 1993", U.S. Department of Justice, Office of Justice Programs, Bureau of Justice Statistics, Washington, D.C.

Table 2. Percentage of prisoners in State and Federal Prisons by Race/Ethnicity and Percent in Population: 1992

Race/Ethnicity	% Prisoners	% Population
White	43.3 %	83.3 %
African American	37.3	12.4
Hispanic	8.1	9.5
Other	5.5	n/a

Source: "Prisoners in 1993," U.S. Department of Justice, Office of Justice Programs, Bureau of Justice Statistics, Washington, D.C.

Table 3. Percent of New Court Commitments, by Offense and
Year of Admission: 1980-1992

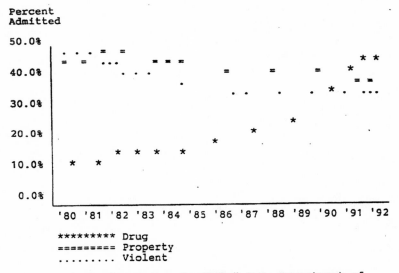

Percent
Admitted

```
50.0%     . . . =  =
          =  =  . . .       ■ ■ ■                              * *
40.0%     =  =  . . .                 =        =       =     *
                    . . .                                      = ■
30.0%                       .           . .      .      . *  . ...
                                                      * 
20.0%                                       .   *
                                    *
10.0%     *     *       * * *    *
0.0%
      '80 '81 '82 '83 '84 '85 '86 '87 '88 '89 '90 '91 '92
```

```
********** Drug
========== Property
.......... Violent
```

Source: "Prisoners in 1993," U.S. Department of
Justice, Office of Justice Programs, Bureau
of Justice Statistics, Washington, D.C.

Table 4. Percentage of Inmates Reporting to Have Ever
Used Drugs: 1991

Any Drug	79 %
Marijuana	74 %
Cocaine/Crack	50 %
Heroin/Opiates	25 %

Source: "Survey of State Prison Inmates: 1991," U.S.
Department of Justice, Office of Justice
Programs, March, 1993, Bureau of Justice
Statistics, Washington, D.C.

7

The recent rise in prison populations and the associated problems of over-crowding, gang violence, drug trafficking and increase in youth offenders are indeed a testimony to the fact that state and federal correctional systems are far from adequate. It is up to social scientists to explain the various reasons for these facts and to arrive at a comprehensive understanding of the various structural elements and organizational dynamics of the system of corrections that may be contributing to the problem. The goal of this study is to examine a prison institution, with its various interrelated patterns of social behavior. The central issues will focus on the various social dynamics which are changing, altering and shaping the normative structure and social organization of the modern prison. It is hypothesized that gang violence, drug-trafficking, overcrowding and an increase in youthful offenders are forces that have had a profound effect on the social structure of the modern prison, and that these forces have come to interplay with one another in a significant way to shape the course of development of penal institutions across the United States. An increasingly violent and uncontrollable population of incarcerated individuals has emerged, along with a system of growing tolerance by staff for rule violation. The long term trend is the production of a class of criminals who are caught up in a cycle of re-involvement in criminal activity, as the wheels of violence, law-breaking activities, and idleness follow the criminal into the prison, behind the wall, into his cell block, and into his cell, penetrating his everyday thoughts, behaviors, and activities.

This work is an effort at understanding the various structural and organizational elements of the modern prison. A current analysis of the prison system is imperative in order to update the literature on prison social organization, in light of changing penal policies, practices and procedures. It is also important to further elaborate upon the structure of imprisonment as empirical research will help to advance the scientific analysis of prison organization and clarify a subject that is too often neglected, misunderstood, distorted and misrepresented.

This research also has important implications for criminal justice policy.

It is necessary to adequately address policy and procedure issues of punishment and corrections according to the demands and needs of the modern prison, as dictated by the various characteristics of its operational structure. It is up to social scientists to provide the significant trends which are constantly emerging among the inmate population, and to arrive at a comprehensive understanding of the various ways in which these trends have come to impact the social organization of the modern prison. Without such current and relevant information, the social forces of change and progress would be annihilated by the potent effects of complacency and ignorance.

My starting point is the sociological perspective of conflict theory. The conflict perspective sees society as divided between competing interests, with wealth and power being unevenly distributed amongst the various members. The conflict perspective is concerned with the constant conflicts and struggles that change and effect the fabric of society. These conflicts are inherent to the structure and arrangement of society (Chambliss, 1973: 3).

Conflict theory argues that, "the central feature of social organization is stratification, the kind and degree of inequality among groups and individuals and their domination over one another" (Ritzer. 1990: 68). The existence of social class and social inequality leads to recurrent conflicts in which the State intervenes in class struggles and creates rules and laws to control threats to the established political, economic and social relations. Coercion is a necessary component in the perpetuation of social inequality, as it is "the chief factor undergirding and maintaining social institutions such as private property, slavery and other institutions which give rise to unequal rights and privileges" (Chambliss, 1973: 4).

Conflict theorists explain society by looking at large social structures and how they dictate the behavior of the various groups and individuals which are a part of this structure. Thus, the forces which drive social change must be studied in light of the various interests of groups and individuals in maintaining their

9

positions of domination. "Who wins in these power struggles depends on the resources controlled by the different factions, including material resources for violence and for economic exchange" (Ritzer, 1990: 68). The analysis of social structure and its impact on the behavior of individuals in society rests upon the shoulders of the Marxist tradition. Marx viewed crime and delinquency as the outcome of the capitalist economic system (Tucker, 1978). The organization of labor under capitalism is such that different social classes have different shares of the goods produced (Tucker, 1978). The resulting pattern is a class struggle between those social classes who try to maintain their high status and those disadvantaged classes who try to better their lot. Accordingly, Marx views crime as "the struggle of the isolated individual against the prevailing conditions" (Marx and Engels, 1968).

Thus, a central feature of law in society, according to the Conflict theoretical perspective, is to maintain and legitimize existing social and economic institutions which operate in the interests of the wealthy ruling class. Marx and Engels write of the wealthy bourgeoisie

> ...the material life of individuals, which by no means depends merely on their will, their mode of production and form of intercourse, which mutually determine each other -this is the real basis of the State and remains so at all stages at which the division of labour and private property are still necessary...the individuals who rule in these conditions, besides having to constitute their power in the form of the State, have to give their will, which is determined by these definite conditions, a universal expression as the will of the State, as Law -an expression whose content is always determined by the relations of this class, as the civil and criminal law demonstrates in the clearest possible way

(Marx and Engels, 1968).

Within this perspective, human beings are seen as having the capacity to do whatever they want. Human nature is creative, and only limited by the extent to which the mind can produce intellectual thought (Tucker, 1978: 160). However, Karl Marx argues that individuals never reap the fruits of their productive potential, as the structure of capitalist society robs them of this potential and leaves them estranged from their labor, their work, their fellow human beings and their own selves. Individuals live a life of alienation, derived from the fact that labor is "external to the worker, ie, it does not belong to his essential being; in his work, therefore, [man] does not affirm himself but denies himself, does not feel content but unhappy, does not develop freely his physical and mental energy but mortifies his body and ruins his mind" (Marx in Tucker, 1978: 74). In reality, people have no control over their own productivity, and in this sense labor is forced or coerced, as the working class is exploited by the capitalists who seek to maximize their profits. From the conflict perspective, it follows that prisons are an important social institution designed to coerce people into accepting existing inequalities and the rules and laws which perpetuate them. Under the capitalist system of economic production in the United States, the laboring segment of the population must be compelled to sell its labor power (Adamson, 1984). In order to increase profits and keep wages down, a portion of the laborers must be excluded from employment to ensure that the laboring population does not withhold its labor. According to Marx, it is the economic structure of society that is the real foundation on which rises legal and political superstructures and to which correspond definite forms of social consciousness...the mode of production in material life determines the general character of the social, political, and spiritual processes of life (Marx, 1904).

Thus, according to the Marxist tradition, capitalist accumulation constantly produces a population which is superfluous to capitals' average requirements for its own valorization and is, therefore, a surplus population (Adamson, 1984). In light of these dynamics, a large portion of criminal populations are recruited from this surplus population of individuals unemployed due to the downward shifts in business and industry. The surplus population are regarded as a potential political threat and a drain on the economic resources of the State (Adamson, 1984). However, Adamson clearly portrays the State as exploiting the presence of this surplus population by

> using criminal populations as a political resource to mobilize commitment to community norms, and as an economic resource, both by extracting surplus value from the labor of prisoners and driving down the wages of employed workers...The processing of populations through the criminal justice system is thus a function of labor supply and the

11

business cycle, depending upon whether the criminal population is seen as a threat to production or as an exploitive economic resource. The extent to which captive criminal populations will be exploited as a resource for capital accumulation is represented as a direct function of the financial strategy of prison reformers, prison administrators and government officials, and as an indirect function of their crime and class control aims (Adamson, 1984).

This approach sheds some important light on the issues of corrections, punishment and imprisonment. Policy outcomes affecting the practices of sentencing and corrections must be understood within the context of their development in response to structural changes in the various social, political and economic institutions of society. Prison policies and procedures are not to be viewed only as remedial reactions to the threat of crime and the demands of crime control. Conflict theorists Georg Rusche and Otto Kirschheimer pointed out in Punishment and Social Structure (1939) the importance of investigating the latent functions of prisons in order to gain an understanding of the ideology underlying the policies which support their existence. They maintain that "we must study the intensity of penal practices as they are determined by social forces, above all by economic and fiscal forces," in order to gain a better understanding of the role which corrections play in meeting the demands and changes of the economic structure (Rusche and Kirschheimer, 1939).

Rusche and Kirschheimer argue that while the rationale for imprisonment stands as significant in its own right, the latent functions of punishment explain more of the variation in its form and frequency. Conflict theory draws upon this insight and proposes that the understanding of correctional policy must be achieved in light of the intervention of power elites (Liska, 1992).

It is arguable that prisons, as presently organized, contribute to rather than decrease the problem of crime and delinquency (Hazelrigg, 1969; DiIulio Jr., 1987; Tonry, 1993). Conflict theories of imprisonment point to the problematic nature of traditional interpretations of penology which maintain that as crime rates rise, the agents in the criminal justice system tend to become more punitive as a way to deter criminals and potential criminals, and thus curb the crime trend. This

12

is notably problematic in light of the empirical evidence that the evolution of penology is not accompanied by a subsequent reduction in criminal behavior (Liska, 1992). The evidence thus demonstrates conflict theory's superiority over arguments presented by alternative theories such as Functionalism. The functionalist perspective views society as a harmonious entity in which ongoing social relations meet existing needs (Chambliss, 1973). Functionalists minimize the existence of social conflict in the various institutions of society; instead, this theoretical approach regards the various governing bodies of society as being neutral and as existing to serve and promote the common good of all (Chambliss, 1973). Social inequality, in the functionalist view, is minimized, and economic advantage is regarded as the product of hard work and personal talent (Chambliss, 1973).

The functionalist paradigm ignores the essential changes in society which occur through the various conflicts and struggles over the organization of social, political and economic institutions (Lopreato, 1972; Domhoff, 1990). Conflict theory presents a more realistic view of society. Social inequality is regarded as being a chief source of social conflict, where opposing interests are reflected in class struggles over the domination of various social institutions (Lopreato, 1972; Chambliss, 1973). Thus, conflict theory accounts for the important dynamic of coercion that is not reflected in functionalist thought, which is seen as the chief factor in the perpetuation and maintenance of unequal rights and privileges in society (Chambliss, 1973). Conflict theories regard the state and its various social control agents, including the criminal justice system, as instruments used by the ruling classes for their own benefit, regardless of the oppressive impacts they may have (Domhoff, 1990). This presents a direct challenge to efforts made by criminologists and other social scientists for a reduction in the criminal justice system, through the reforming and transforming of crime-producing social, political and economic institutions and policies (Lopreato, 1972). There are constant calls for a change in legal statutes toward a decriminalization of policies.

There are solutions presented which express a need for fewer rather than more prisons, as prisons are needed only for the truly dangerous, and not for all offenders. These solutions based upon this philosophy are what have come to be known as alternatives to imprisonment and center upon the idea of de-carceration and community corrections (Hazelrigg, 1969).

However, the failure of the criminal justice system to use alternatives to incarceration can be understood in light of the conflicting and contradictory role they play in the context of the larger social structure and power distribution, for the arrangement of prisons as presently operated serves the private interests of certain segments of society, which far outweighs any effort to reform, rearrange, reduce or eliminate the present system of corrections (Reiman, 1990; Christie, 1993).

Conflict theorist George Vold notes that

> the prohibitionist desires to outlaw the manufacture and sale of alcoholic beverages; the distillers and brewers wish unrestricted opportunity to make and sell a product for which there is a genuine demand; the complicated collection of regulations that American communities know so well, including special taxes, special licensing fees and regulations, special inspections and special rules for closing hours, are all part of the compromise settlement in the clash of these incompatible interests (Vold, 1958: 240).

Likewise, conflict exists in the struggle for competing interests between those who support the law and those who violate it, culminating in the prison treatment of the violators by those who wish to have the law enforced. The scale of compromise is tipped in favor of those who support the law, given their tremendous power relative to social, economic, and political mobility.

The outcome of these dynamics is a system of corrections that is maintained and perpetuated by those powerful forces who support the law, that serves the interests of those same individuals, and that exercises discretion to bring mainly those who are politically powerless into the purview of the law (Christie, 1993). Conflict theorists arguing along these lines take their argument a step further and claim that by "maintain" and "perpetuate", the system of corrections is actually designed to produce and uphold a criminal class in order to sustain that institution which serves the interests of those in power (Reiman, 1990: 5). Thus, it is argued that stricter sentencing measures, increased convictions, and longer sentences, combined with increases in annual state and federal spending for prisons have all worked together to maintain an interest amongst the powerful private sector to keep and even to expand the correctional system as it is presently organized and operated.

Chambliss and Seidman note in Law, Order and Power (1971) that discretion at every level of the criminal justice system "will be so exercised as to bring mainly those who are politically powerless into the purview of the law" (Chambliss and Seidman, 1971). Jeffrey Reiman elaborated this idea in The Rich Get Richer and the Poor Get Prison (1990) by developing what he calls the Pyrric defeat theory (Reiman, 1990). Reiman argues that "the failure of the criminal justice system yields such benefits to those in positions of power that it amounts to success" (Reiman, 1990). Reiman further claims that the criminal justice system is designed to produce a distorted image of the crime problem in American society. Arrest records, court decisions and sentencing convictions are all designed to identify those acts which are dangerous society as primarily the work of the poor, urban black youth population.

However, crime data represent a distorted image of the real crime problem in society, as "we have a greater chance of being killed, or disabled by occupational injury or disease, unnecessary surgery, or by shoddy emergency medical services than by aggravated assault or even homicide" (Reiman, 1990). Yet, the perpetrators of these white-collar crimes rarely become part of the criminal population as reflected in arrest records and prison statistics. Thus, when we look into our prisons, the image we have of what poses a threat to our well-being are the poor, as the wealthy are "weeded out" of the criminal justice process, through its many biased policies, practices and procedures (Reiman, 1990). Thus, the prison system, as presently organized, with its increasing demands to incarcerate more of the "dangerous" members of society, serves to maintain the explicit ideology that the real threat of crime is a threat from the poor (Domhoff, 1990). Reiman expands his theory to explain why current criminal justice policies persist by arguing that the policies fail in a way that does not tend to give rise to an effective demand for change (Reiman, 1990). He concludes by making the argument that

> this failing system provides benefits for those with power to make changes; because the criminal justice system shaped the public's conception of what is dangerous, it creates the impression that the harms it is fighting are the **real** threats to society...thus, even when people see that the system is less than a roaring success, they generally do no more than demand more of the same: more prisons and more prison sentences (Reiman, 1990).

The ideology of corrections, by focusing on the individual acts of the poor, minority groups, has the outcome of diverting the attention away from the various inequalities manifested in our social, political and economic institutions, that have a direct benefit for those in power (Domhoff, 1990; Christie, 1993). By relaying the message that the threat to middle class Americans comes from those below them on the economic ladder, not those above, it deflects the fear and discontent of middle class Americans, and their possible opposition, away from the wealthy ruling classes and legitimizing current power structures within society (Reiman, 1990; Liska, 1992).

A review of the literature indicates that in the late 1950s, the view of prisons as consisting of normatively interlocked roles emerged as the primary theme in criminological research. Gresham M. Sykes pioneered a study of a maximum security facility at the New Jersey State Prison, where he dealt with the convict social organization as a social system composed primarily of an inmate culture and "argot" roles (Sykes, 1958). His work culminated in the 1958 publication of The Society of Captives, and has served as a stimulus and model for sociological research on prison organization for many decades to follow.

Sykes was concerned about the vast misunderstanding and ignorance about the prison as a social system of interrelated patterns of social behavior. "Without a fuller knowledge of the social structure of the prison as a whole," he wrote, "conclusions concerning the causes and effects of particular reactions could be grossly misleading" (Sykes, 1958: xix). Thus, Sykes emphasized the need to study the variety of roles played by inmates and their custodians within the prison environment.

The data for the study were gathered from the following sources: (1) official publications and reports of the Department of Institutions and Agencies for the State of New Jersey; (2) regulations, standard procedure, monthly reports and similar material issued by the Trenton Prison; (3) individual files for the members of the inmate population; (4) tape recorded interviews with inmates; (5) questionnaires concerning inmate behavior, provided by Wing guards and Shop officers; (6) personal observation; and (7) informal interviews with senior officials, guards, and inmates (Sykes, 1958: 135).

Order within a maximum security prison is described by Sykes as emerging from the existing set of relationships that develop to cope with life in captivity, and what is characterized as "the pains of imprisonment" (Sykes, 1958: 63-64). The deprivations or frustrations of prison life include the loss of liberty, goods and services, heterosexual relationships, autonomy, and security. Sykes argued that social scientists must "explore the way in which the deprivations and frustrations pose profound threats to the inmate's personality or sense of personal worth" (Sykes, 1958: 64).

The deprivation of liberty is said to occur through the inmate's confinement to the institution and confinement within the institution (Sykes, 1958). The impact of this deprivation represents "a deliberate, moral rejection of the criminal by the free community; the prisoner is never allowed to forget that, by committing a crime, he has foregone his claim to the status of a full-fledged, trusted member of society" (Sykes, 1958: 65-66).

Likewise, the deprivation of goods and services has profound consequences, as the lack of personal possessions strips the inmate of much of his own self-identity, leaving him to "equate his material deprivation with personal inadequacy" (Sykes, 1958: 70). The deprivation of heterosexual relationships is probably the most frustrating of the pains of imprisonment. An essential component of the inmate's self -his masculinity -is constantly being questioned in a society composed exclusively of men, regardless of whether or not he is being "coerced, bribed, or seduced into an overt homosexual liaison" (Sykes, 1958: 71).

The deprivation of autonomy is seen as the product of the many trivial rules of conduct prescribed by the official custodial agents of the prison (Sykes, 1958). Sykes points out that many of the rules and regulations of the New Jersey State Prison arouse the hostility and anger of prisoners because they simply do not make sense. Thus, he notes, "the frustration of the prisoner's ability to make choices and the frequent refusals to provide an explanation for the regulations and commands descending from the bureaucratic staff involves a profound threat to the prisoner's self-image because they reduce the prisoner to the weak, helpless, dependent status of childhood" (Sykes, 1958: 75).

Finally, Sykes addresses an inmate's deprivation of security as he is placed in the vulnerable position of constantly having to fight for his own safety. He describes the world of thieves, rapists, aggressive homosexuals, and murderers as having a "sufficient number of outlaws within this group of outlaws to deprive the average prisoner of that sense of security which comes from living among men who can be reasonably expected to abide by the rules of society" (Sykes, 1958: 77).

Faced with these pains of imprisonment, the society of captives must find a way to interact amongst each other so as to reduce or mitigate the deprivations they experience from their captivity. Sykes thus explores the system of social roles which arises through the dynamics of interaction in the prison organization. He describes these roles through the language, the "argot," of criminals which serves as an expression of group membership and as a means of organizing and classifying the various experiences of the inmates in dealing with the many problems of life in prison.

The roles contained within the inmate social world are described as being played by "rats," "center men," "gorillas," "merchants," "wolves," "punks," "fags," "ball- busters," "real men," "toughs," and "hipsters" (Sykes, 1958: 106). The patterns of behavior that arise from these various social roles are directly linked to the deprivations and frustrations of confinement to which all inmates must react, respond or adapt themselves. With the exception of the "real man," the social roles represent the attempts by inmates to "reduce the rigors of prison life at the expense of fellow prisoners and the individual pursues his own interests, his own needs, without regard for the needs, rights and opinions of others. Inmate cohesion or solidarity is sacrificed for personal aggrandizement; bonds of mutual loyalty, aid, affection, and respect are subordinated to individualistic ends" (Sykes, 1958: 107). The rare exception to these behavior patterns is the "real man," a term extended to cover social roles which involve "loyalty, generosity, sexual restraint, and the minimizing of frictions among inmates as well as endurance with dignity" (Sykes, 1958: 107).

Sykes concludes his study with the observation that the organization of a prison involves the careful balance of compromise between the rulers and the ruled. He argues that the structure of imprisonment, with its various tasks and demands, cannot operate with total power placed in the hands of the official bureaucracy. Custodial power must give way to the various rules, expectations and values of the convict social system. Thus, in the final analysis, "the effort of the custodians to 'tighten up' the prison undermines the cohesive forces at work in the inmate population and it is these forces which play a critical part in keeping the society of the prison on an even keel" (Sykes, 1958: 124).

The study of prisons as institutions where norms and roles are dictated by the structural and organizational needs and demands of the social system continued throughout the 1960s. In 1961, Donald Cressey published The Prison, which contained various studies in institutional organization and change. This volume was written with the aim of establishing the essential notion that "one who participates in an organization that 'owns' certain kinds of behavior will exhibit those kinds of behavior. Events occur because there is an organizational place for them to occur, and they do not recur when the place is eliminated" (Cressey, 1961: 9).

Cressey highlights the key argument that the explanation of and response to deviant behavior "must show concern for the organizational context in which the behavior occurs, as well as for the traits of the actor" (Cressey, 1961: 7). Thus, studies of social organization of prisons must emphasize the effects of the structure of prisons on the behaviors of inmates and staff. He argues that "the official and unofficial aspects of social organization are important determinants of the behavior, including attitudes, opinions, and beliefs, of the persons participating" (Cressey, 1961: 3).

Another study of institutional organization paralleling that of Cressey was done by Erving Goffman in his classic work Asylums (1961). He defined a total institution as "a place of residence and work where a large number of like-situated individuals, cut off from the wider society for an appreciable period of time, together lead an enclosed, formally administered round of life" (Goffman, 1961: xiii). Goffman spent a year at St. Elizabeth's Hospital in Washington, D.C. doing field research on total institutions. There, through participant observation as an assistant to the athletic director, he learned about "the social world of the hospital inmate, as this world is subjectively experienced by him" (Goffman, 1961: ix).

Goffman was concerned with the inmate's situation (his status and experiences) within the institution and how this could lead to a sociological formulation of the structure of the self. The essential features of total institutions are: (1) all aspects of life are conducted in the same place and under the same single authority; (2) each phase of the member's daily activity is carried on in the immediate company of a large batch of others, all of whom are treated alike and required to do the same thing together; and (3) all phases of the day's activities are tightly scheduled (Goffman, 1961: 6).

Goffman describes the process of entry into a total institution as stripping the inmate of his former identity, as he loses his friends and family, his possessions, and even his name (Goffman, 1961). Entry means a total loss self-autonomy, as the self is violated by the inmate's lack of control over his immediate thought and action. Thus, elaborates Goffman, the inmate "begins a series of abasements, degradations, humiliations, and profanations of self...his self is systematically, if often unintentionally, mortified" (Goffman, 1961: 14). Total control of the inmate's environment - his ability to use the telephone, mail letters, use the bathroom, smoke and spend money, strips him of his right to act on his own as an adult and produces in the inmate "the terror of feeling radically demoted in the age-grading system" (Goffman, 1961: 43).

Within this framework of social organization, there exist a number of means by which inmates learn to cope with the dynamics of confinement in a total institution. Goffman refers to this as a system of secondary adjustment, whereby inmates engage in "practices that do not directly challenge staff but allow inmates to obtain forbidden satisfactions or to obtain permitted ones by forbidden means...these practices are variously referred to as "the angles," "knowing the ropes," "conniving," "gimmicks," "deals," or "ins" (Goffman, 1961: 54). Goffman notes that these patterns reach the epitome of their practice within the prison institution.

Secondary adjustments take many forms. One pattern involves the fraternization of inmates and the collective rejection and mocking of staff (Goffman, 1961: 59). Another line of adaptation involves what Goffman calls "situational withdrawal," where the inmate diverts his attention from everything except those events and situations immediately surrounding his body (Goffman, 1961: 61). Alternatively, an inmate can react to the structure of his confinement through what Goffman describes as "intransigent line." In this situation, the inmate "intentionally challenges the institution by flagrantly refusing to co-operate with staff" (Goffman, 1961: 62). The opposite of this adjustment is "conversion," where the inmate sets out to be the perfect model of institutional behavior by accepting the official view of himself. (Goffman, 1961: 63). Finally, Goffman describes "colonization" as an adaptation, where the inmate comes to view the institution as a "stable, relatively contented existence" (Goffman, 1961: 62). This type of individual comes to reap the maximum benefits possible from within the institutional setting.

The culture of inmates arises out of and is sustained by the various problems of confinement. The conditions of life in total institutions - forced childhood, inability to earn a living, sustain a marital relationship, raise children, and interact with free society - engenders the ideology amongst inmates that time in the institution is time wasted..."it is something that must be 'done' or 'marked' or 'put in' or 'pulled'" (Goffman, 1961" 67). Furthermore, inmates in a total institution are constantly facing an ideology of personal failure and self-pity. Goffman observes that "the low position of inmates relative to their station on the outside, established initially through the stripping processes, creates a milieu of personal failure in which one's fall from grace is continuously pressed home" (Goffman, 1961: 67).

Thus, the behavior patterns of inmates in total institutions must be seen as being a reaction to and product of the structural milieu of which they are forced to become a part of. Once again there is an emphasis on social organization as precipitating various roles that must emerge to cope with social confinement of the individual. Thus, the inmate social system may be viewed as providing a way of life which allows the inmate to avoid the consequences of accepting social rejection and instead create a means by which he rejects the rejectors and not himself (Goffman, 1961: 58). In doing this, he can escape the stigma accorded to his status by society, as an "inmate," a "convict," or a "prisoner," thereby challenging the interpretive scheme that "a man in a political prison must be traitorous; a man in a prison must be a law breaker; a man in a mental hospital must be sick...if not traitorous, criminal, or sick, why else would he be there?"

(Goffman, 1961: 84).

Throughout the 1950s and 1960s, the dominant theme in the sociological and criminological literature was the analysis of the prison community as a social system, with various roles, norms and values arising out of the needs and demands of the structure of the institution. The research findings painted a picture of a system which fostered an entire inmate sub-culture that attempted to deal with the problems of adjustment to life in prison. In 1940, Donald Clemmer coined the term "prisonization" in his famous study of prison culture, The Prison Community. Clemmer defined prisonization as "the process of assimilation of the prison culture by inmates as they become acquainted with the prison world" (Clemmer, 1958: 299). Essentially, when an inmate first enters the prison institution, he is stripped of all forms of self identity. He is no longer allowed to attach meaning to personal objects which are symbolic of his own self. He becomes faceless and anonymous, a number without his own identity and personality.

Faced with this reality, the inmate is forced to attach new meanings to the environment he is now a part of, behind prison walls. These new meanings or symbols of personal identity are provided by the prison culture in which "every inmate is exposed to the universal factors of prisonization" (Clemmer, 1958: 299-300) Clemmer identifies several conditions which heighten or maximize the effects of prisonization. These include (1) a lengthy sentence which in turn exposes the inmate to a long-term subjection to the universal factors of prisonization; (2) the unstable personality of an inmate who was unable to make adequate social relations before commitment and a general lack of positive relationships before entry into prison; (3) a readiness to integrate into and form intimate relations with a prison primary group; (4) a blind acceptance of the codes and dogmas of the primary group and the prison population in general; and (5) a willing attitude towards the participation in gambling activities and abnormal sex behavior (Clemmer, 1958).

Thus, the effect of the process of prisonization on the inmate is to make him conform to and become a part of the norms and expectations of the prison culture and to adopt behavior patterns that are contradictory to those expected by free society, once he is released from prison. As Clemmer pointed out, " the influence of the universal factors are sufficient to make a man characteristic of the penal community and probably so disrupt his personality that a happy adjustment in any community becomes next to impossible" (Clemmer, 1958: 300).

In 1961, Donald Garrity elaborated on the work of Clemmer by researching the effects of prisonization. In "The Prison as a Rehabilitation Agency" (1961), Garrity attempted to expand the literature on prisons by arguing that "there is a general consensus that prison experience is criminogenic in nature; prisons breed crime...exposing an individual to experience in prison increases the probability that he will engage in criminal behavior" (Garrity, 1961: 361). Garrity conducted an empirical analysis on a population of inmates released from two Washington prisons over approximately one year. (Garrity, 1961: 365). A total of 1,265 men released on parole were examined. Garrity discovered that an inmate's behavior once paroled depended on the role he played while in prison, and the subjective experiences attached to that role. Garrity uses Schrag's typology of inmate roles -"square john," "right guy," "outlaw," "politician," and "ding," to classify inmates' success or failure on parole (See Clarence C. Schrag, Social Types in a Prison Community, Unpublished M.A. thesis, Univ. of Washington, 1944). Garrity found that the parole violation rate could be predicted on the basis of the person's prison role. The parole violation rate for the "square John" was very low. This was as expected, as his role in prison was characterized by learning compliant role behavior and being pro-social (Garrity, 1961: 376). The "right guy," who was the dominant figure in prison, represented the epitome of the inmate social system, internalizing its various anti-social attitudes and values. As expected, Garrity found that the rate of parole violation was very high for inmates who played this role while incarcerated (Garrity, 1961: 378). The "outlaw" in

24

prison experiences no meaningful relationships in prison and has no attachments either in prison or outside of prison. This type of individual, who neither learns organizational roles nor develops reference group bonds, also has a high rate of parole violation (Garrity, 1961: 378). The "politician" is the individual in prison who is able to conform to the demands of any situation. Thus, it was found that this type of person had few parole violations if his sentence was not long, but the rate of violation increased with the length of his incarceration. This was found to be the case because continued exposure to the prison culture gave the politician more opportunity to conform to the norms and values of anti-social groups which would prove detrimental to successful performance on parole (Garrity, 1961: 377). Finally, the category "ding," relegated to alienated individuals who are shunned by other prisoners, was divided into several sub-types of roles. It was found that "dings" who were either pro-social as the "square John" or who were mentally deficient, had very low violation rates on parole. The homosexual "ding," who is exposed to and becomes involved in a violent homosexual environment while imprisoned, experiences a high rate of parole violation (Garrity, 1961: 279).

Thus, Garrity argues that the claim that prisons are "breeding grounds for crime and that imprisonment adversely affects all prisoners" must be qualified by the fact that the effects of the prison experience on inmates "vary according to the roles assigned to inmates by other inmates and by the staff" (Garrity, 1961: 378-379). Garrity's study is complemented by the concerns expressed by John Irwin in The Felon (1970). Irwin argued that current prison research is not suited to produce a full understanding of the extended career of the felon. Thus, he set out to investigate the prison organization and the convict's social world "with an eye toward post prison behavior" (Irwin, 1970: 61). He conducted a study at the California Department of Corrections where he entered the California prisons to interview inmates, attend pre-parole functions, study the inmate files, interview parole agents and parole administrators, and attend all other parole functions. A total of 116 convicts were studied (Irwin, 1970: 4). Irwin identified three prison adaptive modes that inmates follow which have an impact on their extended career once released from prison. The first he calls "doing time" and is characteristic of the inmate who tries to "maximize his comfort and luxuries and minimize his discomfort and conflict and to get out as soon as possible" (Irwin, 1970: 68). Inmates who become a part of this adaptive mode are usually involved in a number of positive activities in prison and form friendships with other inmates.

"Jailing" is the type of adaptation to prison life whereby the inmate cuts himself off from the outside world and attempts to construct a life within the prison. This type of inmate will "seek positions of power, influence and sources of information, [they] are called 'shots,' 'politicians,' 'merchants,' 'hoods,' 'toughs,' 'gorillas,' or something else..." (Irwin, 1970: 74). For this individual, the environment around him represents a world where arguments are settled by knife and fist and friendships and cliques are means of survival and protection.

Finally, "gleaning" is an adaptation to prison made by those individuals who are looking to better themselves in order to change their identities once released from prison. These inmates take advantage of educational, vocational training and treatment programs and opportunities within the prison in order to improve themselves (Irwin, 1970: 76). Irwin found that the convict identity is central to the future career of the felon. This value or belief system develops through the commitment to a convict code, a "life commitment to do your own time; that is, to live and let live, and when you feel that someone is not letting you live, to either take it, leave, or stop him yourself, but never call for help from official agencies of control" (Irwin, 1970: 83). Irwin notes that it is this identity that poses a threat and barrier to the convict's ability to reorient himself to free society, and influences the choices he makes for many years. Irwin emphasizes the importance of the convict identity to the inmate by arguing that the identity of the old con - the perspectives, the values and beliefs, and other personality attributes which are acquired after the years of doing time, such as advanced age, adjustment to prison routines, and complete loss of skills required to carry on the normal activities of civilians - will usually make living on the outside impossible (Irwin, 1970: 84- 85).

The few inmates who do escape this cycle of failure, stigma and recidivism, notes Irwin, are those offenders who make a final termination of their criminal careers and become immersed in a new world of meanings, friendships, associations activities, and relationships (Irwin, 1970: 203).

A decade after his publication of The Felon, John Irwin pursued the study of prisons with a concern for understanding what actually goes on behind the walls of prisons to the inmates there. Thus, in Prisons in Turmoil (1980), he attempts to "demonstrate that the distorted conceptions of the prison world and of prisoners previously held or manufactured by prison administrators, guards, politicians, and experts function to serve the interests of these (not necessarily the interests of society), and result in pain and unfairness to prisoners" (Irwin, 1980: xiii).

Irwin describes public sentiments in the late 1970s as being characterized by a fear of crime and hostility toward criminals (Irwin, 1980: 139). During this time, there was an emphasis on punitive penal philosophy, with custody, control and discipline of prisoners taking primary precedence in corrections policy. Thus, the modern prison, armed with policies and practices that are designed to thwart inmate activity and obliterate convict unity, faces the unprecedented growth of convicts who detest, resent, mistrust, and attack other prisoners and the prison administration itself (Irwin, 1980: 193).

The social organization of the modern prison is described by Irwin as being in a state of division, tension and hostility, with the "hate and distrust between white and black prisoners constituting the most powerful source of division" (Irwin, 1980: 183). Prisoners tend to form violent cliques and gangs who regularly rob and attack other prisoners for the purpose of retaliating, obtaining goods, gaining respect from fellow prisoners, and seeking sexual favors.

Accordingly, the new prison "hero" is that inmate who is tough, who is "able to take care of [himself] in the prison world where people will attack others with little or no provocation...and [has] the guts to take from the weak" (Irwin, 1980: 193).

Irwin attributes the escalation of murderous gangs, violence and attack in the modern prison partially to a disillusionment on the part of prisoners with the system of corrections. The rehabilitation ideal, with its attributes of cooperation, tolerance and leadership, is replaced by a convict identity that fosters a deep antagonism to the prison administration, with its harsh, punitive approach, which is seen now as the oppressor, the captor and the enemy (Irwin, 1980: 193).

Prisoners who match the ideal convict identity come to control the inmate contraband distribution system. Irwin describes the economic activity of inmate social organization as becoming "much more complex and extensive and interlaced with the clique and gang activity" (Irwin, 1980: 206). The deprivation of legally obtained material goods, whether due to their unavailability or due to inmates' lack of monetary funds, forces almost all inmates to become a part of the illegal goods markets. Today more than ever, prison contraband goes beyond material goods to include a variety of drugs, alcohol, and weapons (Irwin, 1980: 208). Many of these items are smuggled into the prison by friends and relatives during visits, and by guards and other employees working inside the prison.

Irwin describes the contraband system as having changed drastically due to the emerging dynamics of convict relations. Distribution of illegal goods and services has been previously described in the literature as being controlled by a few individuals (usually referred to as "merchants" -see Sykes, 1958: 106). However, the situation now has changed with the emergence of prison gangs and as the "convict ideal shifted toward toughness and rapaciousness: 'racketeers' replaced merchants...racketeers operate in groups and rob as well as sell to other prisoners; with their appearance, the individual entrepreneur faded or disappeared" (Irwin, 1980: 211).

The expansive literature and research on penal institutions throughout the past thirty years is conclusive as to the impact of the culture of the prison institution on its social and structural organization. With prisoner social organization being increasingly marked by a culture of violence, terror, division and tension, administrators are constantly in search for new formulas for the efficient handling of the growing population of inmates. However, for reasons not quite distinctly elaborated, politicians, administrators, and prison officials continue to use, apply and expand old formulas and failed ideas in the attempt to restore order. This is further compounded by emerging trends calling for longer sentences, harsher penalties, and mandatory minimums, resulting in an explosion in prison population. Recent studies on prison social organization have emerged in the works of Lockwood, DiIulio, Marquart, Fleisher, Jacobs and others, which examine the prison institution in the mid to late 1980s. They attempt to identify emerging patterns of convict behavior and their relation to the structural operation of the prison. The current literature on prisons focuses on the dynamics of interaction within the institutional setting, with special attention to the formal and informal relations that emerge and develop between inmates and staff and their impact on the structure and organization of correctional operation and management.

Thus, current studies attempt to evaluate and explain the prevalence and impact of violence, rape, drugs, overcrowding, gang activity, brutality and various other dynamics of the prison setting. This study will attempt to complement, synthesize and expand the current literature on the social organization of the modern prison. Throughout the text, I will draw upon the various insights, observations and findings of previous studies, in order to develop a more comprehensive understanding of the dynamics of prison organization, in light of recent trends in penal policy and legislation. I will attempt to link the elements of criminal justice policy and prison administration, with the various emergent roles, structures and relations that exist between inmates and staff within the prison

29

system, and the effects these dynamics have on crime as a whole. I intend to put my observations within the context of the larger socio-political, economic structure within which prisons are organized and operated, which is rarely mentioned in prison literature and research.

In order to approach the task of field research within a prison environment, it is necessary to examine a comprehensive array of data in order to fulfill the goals of the qualitative task at hand. Throughout this study, different aspects of the prison experience were studied, observed and analyzed. The goal of this research was to analyze the social organization of the modern prison. A formal social organization is theoretically defined as "a large, complex group that is deliberately created to achieve certain goals" (Maris, 1988: 97). Formal organizations are usually characterized by a division of labor, a set of interrelated and specialized tasks. In every formal organization, there exists a formal and informal structure, necessary for the effective operation of the organization.

The formal structure is deliberately designed and implemented to accomplish certain goals. However, informal practices emerge which become incorporated into and sometimes even change the formal structure of the organization. The informal structure consists of "patterns of interaction, friendships, personal behavior, 'common knowledge,' and informal authority, which differ from the practices specified in the rules and procedures of the organization" (Maris, 1988: 98). Thus, the "real" structure of an organization includes both formal rules and informal practices.

The major indicators of this theoretical construct must therefore "tap" both the formal and informal structure of the prison. Accordingly, the social organization of the prison must be studied with a comprehensive understanding of the various aspects of the prison experience. This includes 1) formal organizational operation, defined as institutional goals, rules, procedures and practices, and 2) organizational patterns of interaction, defined as inmate-inmate relations, inmate-staff relations, and staff- staff relations. This study was therefore designed to test the impact of the developing social dynamics of prison overcrowding, gang activities, drug trafficking and increase in youthful offenders on the organizational operation and patterns of interaction of the modern prison institution.

The data for this research were gathered from various resources, including (1) a six month study conducted at the Central facility, Lorton Correctional Complex, D.C. Department of Corrections, from March 1994 to August 1994; and (2) weekly attendance at the Ex-offenders Task Force meeting during the same six month period, held at Shiloh Baptist Church in Washington D.C. The study is based upon several techniques of field research, of which the first and foremost is the in-depth interview. Interviews were conducted with 100 inmates, 50 correctional officers, covering all ranks, and 30 program coordinators and institutional administrators, including staff psychologists, case workers, unit managers, lieutenants, captains, program directors and the warden. The average length of an interview was approximately 20 minutes. However, this does not include the many one minute remarks, comments and conversations with inmates and staff, that were recorded on a daily basis. Interviews were initiated and set up using both convenient and snowball sampling. The most basic technique involved approaching individuals and asking them if they could spend a few minutes with me. Sometimes, someone would tell me to speak to"so and so" who has a whole lot of knowledge about the prison system, at which time I would set up an interview with that individual. Often, though, inmates and staff would approach me where ever I was and ask me what I was doing. After I would tell them I am doing research on the social organization of prisons, they would begin giving me information about their own experiences and observations. I believe that being a female researcher in the correctional setting worked to my advantage as this was sufficient to make most inmates and some male correctional officers want to stop and talk with me...about anything.

The content of the interviews focused on the issues and variables involved in the study - overcrowding, gang activities, drug trafficking and increase in youth offenders - with an attempt to identify their role in the development of the social organization of the prison. A wide array of topics was covered in the interviews with inmates and staff, including violence in prison, homosexuality, racketeering activities, drugs, social and personal deprivation, job stress, relations between staff and inmates (especially sexual relations), routine activities and experiences of prison life, corruption among staff, efforts at rehabilitation, administrative roles, inmate social roles and informal relations and much more. Several interviews were conducted with inmate representative organizations, including the Office of Public Defender Service/prisoner rights at Lorton, the Office of Religious and Volunteer Services and C.U.R.E. (Citizens United for the Rehabilitation of Errants). I spoke with eight representatives of the various organizations. At least two interviews were conducted with each individual. Whenever possible, interviews were tape recorded; information was otherwise documented carefully through note-taking.

A second technique of tremendous importance is participant observation in inmate activities. The administration allowed me a lot of freedom to participate in such activities as dining with the inmates during lunch, joining religious activities such as prayer meetings, bible studies and choir practice, participating in sports/games during inmate-staff picnics, working side by side with inmates in industries, attending inmate meetings for sharing common grievances, and sharing in and observing educational, vocational and rehabilitation programs. I also spent several days interacting with inmates in their dormitories -listening to music, reading, talking, doing laundry, etc. Interaction took place twice a week for about four hours each time. As in other qualitative studies of prisons, I hope that these data gathering procedures will allow me to arrive at a comprehensive analysis of the formal and informal organization of the modern prison by actually "living through" the experience of incarceration, with specific attention to the tensions and problems associated with overcrowding, gang violence, drug trafficking and increase in youthful offenders. It must be noted however that regardless of my close interaction with inmates, I cannot claim to have had the full experience of being incarcerated. Without actually being an inmate, there is no way to experience the full range and intensity of life inprison. Also, an important source of data comes from the weekly interaction with inmates at the Ex-offenders Task Force Meeting. This part of the research was essential in identifying the long-term effects of incarceration on patterns of reinvolvement in criminal activities. Although this aspect of my data was limited by the fact that there was no extensive, long-term follow-up of the inmates released from prison, it was nevertheless important in putting the research in perspective with regard to the many problems, hardships and obstacles that inmates socialized into prison life experience once they are released back into society.

It is essential that data obtained from interviews and observations be supplemented and cross-checked with other data, such as formal documents. Information was obtained from various official reports and publications of the D.C. Department of Corrections. This includes regulations, standard operating procedures, goals, programs and activities, case histories of inmates, incidences of violence of inmates against each other and against staff, and incidences of abuse/negligence of staff against inmates. Information is also obtained on nutritional standards, medical adequacy, housing accommodations, and recreational facilities.

The population of interest in this study is the population of all inmates and staff at state correctional institutions in the United States. The study was limited to a single state correctional institution, the D.C. Department of Corrections, and focuses primarily upon the inmates and staff at the Central Facility, a higher medium security institution at the Lorton Correctional Complex. This facility has a population of approximately 1,600 inmates.

Several issues must be highlighted with regard to the limitations of such a study, as I have designed it. First and foremost is the issue of personal safety. I had the complete freedom to move around the prison, to go anywhere and to interview and observe anyone. Because this facility houses predominantly individuals with felony convictions and with violent criminal histories, it was necessary at first to be escorted throughout the facility by a staff member, usually a correctional officer. However, I must emphasize that I was at no time threatened or placed in a situation of imminent danger. I learned to control my anxieties, look everyone in the eye and appear to be confident, relaxed and unshakable. However, I had to balance out this presentation of self without appearing to be arrogant, suspicious and unfriendly.

This brings to light another problem, that of trust. Seeing me escorted by a staff member can cause the inmates to identify me with the "authorities," and therefore be reluctant to disclose certain facts. This can be compounded by the fact that I am a stranger and a researcher, who is constantly observing them. However, trust is something that I earned from the inmates. After a few weeks at Central, I began to become familiar with the facility and began to be at ease with being there. At the risk of personal safety, I decided to move throughout the compound without being escorted by a staff member, especially correctional officers, during my interaction with inmates in the mess hall, dormitories, the infirmary, chapel, industries and gymnasium. I told the assistant warden, who expressed concern, that this was absolutely necessary in order to remove a major obstacle to my research, namely, the close presence of a correctional officer during my interviews. After a period of argument and consideration, she allowed me to do this as long as I gave a detailed account of where I was going and what time I would be there. So, the administration always knew where I was; I could always hear them on their radios, relaying information back and forth, "the student is coming...the student is going...open the gate for the student". My tensions were eventually overcome and I began to relax a little, even become familiar with certain faces, activities and events. The inmates in general acted differently now that my presence usually did not also include the presence of staff. They were more themselves, relaxed, knowing that they wouldn't "get a shot" (a disciplinary report) for doing or saying certain things. Now, the inmates would stop and stare, but they always seemed to go back to what they were doing. I learned to ignore and laugh away obscene comments, stares and proposals for marriage. However, I always kept in mind the advice I got from several staff members, to never forget the fact that I was in a prison, surrounded by dangerous individuals. To further gain the trust of inmates who may be suspicious of "research", I tried, as did Jacobs in his study at Stateville (1977), to portray myself as a "volunteer" who is concerned about the state of corrections, and who is looking for ways to improve upon something and someone whom society has given up on. I even became a member of the Office of Religious and Volunteer Services at Lorton and I often wore my I.D. card on my jacket. Thus, the inmates defined my role as an advocate of prison reform. This approach seemed to be more positive than that of Fleisher who became a guard and ran into trouble with the problem of bias against the inmates (Fleisher, 1989). Note taking was also done carefully so as not to seem presumptuous but rather concerned and interested in the individual. Also, all individuals I spoke to, whether staff or inmates, were assured of complete anonymity, as no names whatsoever would be directly referred to in the text. I also had to gain the trust of the staff at the facility, who are constantly being bombarded with negative reports, exposes, and law suits. Putting their job on the line for the sake of a student is not something that most people would do. I had to avoid taking sides in personal disputes and competing factions, and maintain a careful balance between extreme neutrality and becoming emotionally involved with my subjects.

Finally, there was always the lingering and haunting problem of validity in the observational and interview data. Why should I believe the words of a convicted felon who has nothing to lose by lying? I tried to overcome this limitation through the careful understanding of prisoner culture and language. I had to have an accurate knowledge of the individual I am speaking to and understand his motives for saying certain things. I did this by trying to interact with more than one inmate at a time and watch their eyes and body language to see their reactions to each others' comments. Whenever possible, I looked into the record of inmates I interviewed. From these records, I could obtain information on the inmate's childhood experiences, educational achievements, psychological tests and disposition reports. It was also important to collect information in a setting that is comfortable for the inmate or staff member, to avoid the fear of having someone listen to what he or she is saying. I also relied heavily on the information obtained from "old-timers," inmates who have been part of the prison system for several years. These individuals were very knowledgeable with regard to prison organization and eventually became key informants. They also helped to serve as a point of comparison for some of the information given to me by other inmates. Ultimately, however, I had to, as did Sykes, Irwin, Jacobs, Fleisher and others, rely on a keen awareness of my social environment, and the careful eye of personal observation.

CHAPTER 2: HISTORICAL OVERVIEW OF PRISONS

A historical analysis of the development of imprisonment must emphasize the movements and conditions which inspired and brought about major changes in the ideology and structure of imprisonment. Misconceptions about the origins and development of prisons throughout the history of corrections arise from a lack of awareness of the various social and political movements that brought about major changes in the structure of punishment. In order to have a comprehensive understanding of the treatment of offenders in modern penal institutions, it is necessary to understand the significance of historical trends, events and ideologies that shaped the developmental course of prison structure today.

"It has that 'institutional' look shared by police stations, hospitals, orphan asylums, and similar public buildings - a kafka-like atmosphere compounded of naked electric lights, echoing corridors, walls encrusted with the paint of decades, and the stale air of rooms shut up too long" (Sykes, 1968: 7). To most people, the term "prison" represents the laws' reaction to and threat against wrongdoers. It is a symbol of revenge and retribution against those who have sinned against society. It is a means of isolating those who are a threat to our own welfare. Throughout the history of penology, punishment by the state has at all times been motivated by desires to intimidate the criminal, inflict suffering upon him, deter him and others from crime, and protect society (Irwin, 1980). Historically, before the creation of prisons, these aims were thought to be best achieved by corporal and capital punishment. Although jails existed, they were not used for punitive purposes, but instead as a place for detaining offenders held for trial or convicted criminals

37

awaiting the execution of the death penalty. Thus, the criminal codes of the early American colonists relied heavily on corporal and capital punishment. Crimes that did not warrant corporal punishment or death were usually punished by the imposition of fines, especially for the rich. Death was inflicted in numerous ways, including hanging, stoning, and burning at the stake (Pray, 1987). In Pennsylvania between 1718 and 1776, under the British penal code, execution could be prescribed for high treason, petty treason, murder, burglary, rape, sodomy, malicious maiming, manslaughter by stabbing, witchcraft by conjuration, and arson (Pray, 1987). Other crimes were dealt with by imposing corporal punishment, which was designed to terrorize offenders and hold them up to ridicule and shame. Commonplace punishments included the stocks and the pillory, branding of the hand or forehead, public lashes, and public flogging (Irwin, 1980).

However, a shift in penal philosophy began to take place towards the end of the 1700s. People began to perceive the old penal code as barbaric, inhumane, and ineffective, while emphasizing the need for more civilized forms of punishment (Pray, 1987). Several factors seemed to contribute to these ideological changes. Important among these factors were the new ideas brought about by social thinkers of the Enlightenment such as Baron de Montesquieu, Voltaire, Thomas Paine, and Cesare Beccaria. Whereas Calvinists regarded man as being basically depraved the Enlightenment thinkers saw him as being essentially good. Thus, it followed that an individual criminal offender could be reformed or rehabilitated. The work of the Italian criminologist Cesare Beccaria had a profound effect on criminal punishment in the United States and all over the world. Beccaria wrote that "the purpose of punishment is not to torment a sensible being or to undo a crime but is none other than to prevent the criminal from doing injury to society and to prevent others from committing the like offenses" (Beccaria, 1963: 30-33). He called for the abolition of secret accusations and torture to extract confessions. Instead, he urged that accused criminals be treated like human beings and be allowed the opportunity to present evidence in their own defense. He condemned the overly harsh and unequally applied laws as causing more problems than providing solutions. Beccaria wrote that "the severity of the punishment of itself emboldens men to commit the very wrong it is supposed to prevent. They are driven to commit additional crimes to avoid the punishment...the certainty of a punishment, even if it be moderate, will always make a stronger impression than the fear of another which is more terrible but combined with the hope of impunity" (Beccaria, 1963: 30-33). Therefore, Beccaria's solution was to make punishments fit specific crimes. His writings impacted this country so much that by the early 1800s most states had amended their criminal codes and strictly limited the death penalty to the most serious crimes.

The largest contribution to criminal justice reform came from the Quakers in Pennsylvania (Trestar, 1981). As a religious group, they were unable to reconcile the existing brutal criminal punishments with their Christian beliefs. In 1786, they persuaded the Pennsylvania legislature to reserve the death penalty for only the most serious crimes: murder, treason, rape, and arson. Other offenses such as robbery, sodomy, and burglary were punishable by up to ten years in jail. The Quakers also attacked the terrible conditions in jails. In 1787, the Quakers and their supporters formed the Philadelphia Society for Alleviating the Miseries of Public Prisons (Trestar, 1981). The society persuaded the Pennsylvania legislature to convert a jail on Walnut Street into a prison for the confinement of convicted criminals throughout the state. The more serious offenders were to be housed in sixteen solitary cells while the less serious ones were to be kept in large rooms and were to work together in shops. Thus the birth of the first prison as we know it. The most distinguishing characteristic of this Pennsylvania system was the solitary confinement of prisoners 24 hours a day in order for them to reflect on their crimes and become penitent and converted. The initial results of the Walnut Street prison were somewhat promising. Yearly commitments dropped by 75%

from 1789 to 1793. Fewer crimes were being committed and fewer discharged prisoners were being rearrested for new crimes. The Walnut Street prison served as a model for the building of other prisons like it across the United States for the next thirty years.

However, despite the initial enthusiasm over the Walnut Street prison, conditions soon deteriorated. Behavioral difficulties with uncooperative prisoners led to a gradual upsurge of the corporal punishments the prison was designed to eliminate. Overcrowding led to problems in management, financial expenditure, and control. By the early 1800s Walnut Street and other prisons like it were gruesome places (Pray, 1987). Furthermore, the assumption of the Quakers that criminals if left alone would repent for their sins and become good citizens came to be seen as naive. Most prisoners on the contrary went mad and some even died due to horrid conditions and the extreme deprivation of prolonged solitary confinement (Pray, 1987). A prison established in 1790 in an abandoned Coppermine at Simsbury, Connecticut is described by prison historian Richard Phelps:

> the horrid gloom of this dungeon can scarcely be realized. The impenetrable vastness supporting the awful mass above impending as if ready to crush one to atoms; the dripping water trickling like tears from its sides, the unearthly unearthly echoes, all conspired to strike aghast with amazement and horror (Phelps in Pray, 1987).

By 1817, the degenerate conditions of the Pennsylvania- style prison led inevitably to a cry for change.

The situation in New York before the 1790s had been similar to that in Pennsylvania with regard to crime and punishment. Prisons built after the Walnut Street model ran into the same problems of overcrowding and degeneration. Thus, in 1816, a very different prison system was authorized at Auburn, New York, and became known as the "congregate system" (Spierenburg, 1987). This system emphasized common activities, external discipline, hard labor, and forced rehabilitation. This scheme divided prisoners into three classes: the worst offenders were put in solitary confinement, the second class was put in separate cells three days a week, and minor offenders were allowed to work together six days a week. Like the Pennsylvania system, the Auburn system intended to reform the criminal, but instead of solitary soul-searching, the reform was to occur through an emphasis on obedience, order, rigidity, and a regimentation of prison life. This system has continued to serve as the basic model for prisons today. A characteristic feature of the Auburn prison that epitomized order and rigidity was the "lock-step", whereby inmates lined up behind one another in single file with their faces turned down to prevent conversation. The lock- step survived until the 1930s (Spierenburg, 1987).

However, with the passage of time, the new prisons modeled after the Auburn system, like their Walnut Street predecessors, began to deteriorate. The major reason for this pattern was overcrowding. Sentences were not only very long, but were also for a fixed time, with no provisions for early release. The consequence of over- crowding was a relaxation of regulations which in turn enabled inmates to begin communicating with one another and interact freely. The efforts by wardens to maintain order once again brought back the forms of brutality once condemned by prison reformers (Spierenburg, 1987). Prisoners were chained, strapped down, flogged, and otherwise physically restrained. Inmate labor was also misused and abused by private contractors. Accordingly, by the late 1800s, concern over the problems pervading prisons was once again on the rise, and a new wave of penal reform was in the making.

The early twentieth century was marked by the development of a new set of cultural perspectives and ideologies. The emerging field of psychology fostered the theory that it was possible to measure specific personal qualities. Thus came the idea of assessing the causes of criminality in individual offenders and treating each one accordingly, in much the same way a physician would treat a sick patient (Trestar, 1981). This "medical model" approach allowed prison administrators considerable discretion in deciding how to treat and when to release a convict. The offspring of reform movements during this era was the use of indeterminate sentencing. This practice allowed a judge to sentence an offender to a time period marked by a minimum and maximum number of years and thus left the actual time of release up to a prison authority, based upon the offender's criminal history and behavior in prison. Indeterminate sentencing was based on the "Irish System" of early release devised in the mid-1800s by Scottish Captain Alexander Maconochie (Trestar, 1981). Correctional administrators embraced the idea of indeterminate sentencing as it would put the fate of offenders in their own hands: early release for hard work and good behavior; prolonged sentence for poor performance. An outgrowth of the indeterminate sentence was the concept of parole. Parole was a time in which the unserved part of the prison sentence was a testing period for the released inmate: if they behaved themselves and kept out of trouble, they were allowed to remain in society, if not, they were put back into prison. Probation was another major development which became a common courtroom disposition between 1900 and 1920. Under probation, the sentencing judge suspends incarceration and instead puts the offender under the supervision of a probation supervisor or agent. If the offender does well during the period of supervision, he or she stays free; if not, the original term of imprisonment is imposed. This practice was advocated by reformers as a way of both reducing prison overcrowding, and meeting the needs of individual offenders. Efforts to encourage visitation and correspondence also became prevalent as the notions of silence and isolation became repugnant and outmoded. Inmates began to be treated as social creatures, as prisons began to provide them with entertainment such as movies, exercise equipment, libraries, and commissary privileges. Also, prisons were equipped with "diagnostic" centers for the testing and evaluating of prisoners and their individual problems in an effort to provide specific treatments (Trestar, 1981).

However, during the 1960s, the common practices of parole, probation, and indeterminate sentencing came under attack. Political ideology shifted towards a "get-tough" attitude towards crime. As described by Legal Historian

Stephen A. Saltzburg, "people looked upon parole as really being a backdoor way around serious punishment for serious offenses" (Saltzburg, 1993). Legislators thus moved to mandate fixed sentences and establish strict guidelines for parole and probation, in an effort to get more criminals into prisons and for longer stays. At the same time, prisoners became more vocal, demanding more rights and privileges and more humane treatment. A 1964 Supreme Court decision gave state prisoners the right to challenge state prison practices in federal court. Dissatisfaction with the uncertainties of indeterminate sentencing and the rehabilitation model led to the proliferation of determinate and mandatory sentences during the 1970s (Haas and Alpert, 1991). On January 30, 1978, Congress adopted a bill proposed by the National Commission on Reform of Federal Criminal Laws that was the culmination of several attempts to impose restrictions on Federal Judges' discretion to use indeterminate sentencing, through the use of presumptive sentencing. Under presumptive sentencing, "the discretion of a judge who imposes a prison sentence is constrained by a specific sentence length set by law for each offense or class of offenses. That sentence must be imposed in all unexceptional cases. In response to mitigating or aggravating circumstances, the judge may shorten or lengthen the sentence within specified boundaries, usually with written justification being required" (Haas and Alpert, 1991: 31).

Trends in the Reagan, Bush and Clinton administrations perpetuate a "lock-em-up and throw away the key" philosophy which calls for more prisons to house all criminals for longer sentences (Saltzburg, 1993). U.S. Supreme Court Justice Warren Burger, who served as Chief Justice of the Supreme Court from 1969 to 1986, epitomized this notion when he asked the following question: "I put to you this question: is a society redeemed if it provides massive safeguards for accused persons including pre-trial freedom for most crimes, defense lawyers at public expense, trials, and appeals, retrials and more appeals, almost without end, and yet fails to provide elementary protection for its decent, law-abiding citizens?" (Eitzen, 1985). Saltzburg argues that many of the problems associated with contemporary prisons -overcrowding, violence, drug trafficking - are indirect results of current ideology of justice and fairness which has become "too caught up with wanting to punish everybody" (Saltzburg, 1993). Indeed, the "get tough on crime" propaganda issued by legislators and political leaders has had a profound impact on the dynamics of prison organization. Determinate sentencing laws have established very long mandatory sentences which have resulted in rapidly increasing incarceration rates. Accordingly, between 1980 and 1990, "the number of sentenced inmates per 100,000 residents rose from139 to 293, representing an 111 percent increase during this period" (Cohen, 1991: 1).

Irwin further notes that not only will prison populations continue to grow, but they will also change in composition, with persons serving time for violent crimes - murder, assault, rape, robbery and burglary -filling up the prisons (Irwin, 1980: 228). Because of the distribution of these crimes in society and the bias in criminal justice procedures -policing, courts and sentencing, the percentages of non-white prisoners will also grow rapidly. Irwin makes the chilling argument that

> these prisoners are the most embittered, aggressive and accustomed to struggling in oppressive situations, such as youth prisons and cities' slums...these prisoners are not getting along with each other. Different races, territorial cliques (home boys), criminal tips, and gangs hate and distrust each other; embittered and aggressive prisoners will not strike back in highly organized fashion, but will continue to operate devious contraband systems, wage war on each other, and occasionally and spontaneously assault staff" (Irwin, 1980: 228-229).

Against this background, I wish to turn now to an examination of the social organization of the modern prison. Throughout the remainder of this study, I wish to portray the prison as a miniature society operating within the structure and context of the society we all participate in on a daily basis. It is easy to think of prisoners as isolates, outcasts, or non-functioning members of our own society. However, we must erase this image completely from our minds if we are to understand the prison institution as merely a reflection, extension and part of society as we know it, live in it, like it, and dislike it.

CHAPTER 3: OVERVIEW OF LORTON CENTRAL PRISON

Lorton Prison is a complex of seven separate institutions. The largest is the Central facility, composed of a heterogeneous population of offenders, with diverse criminal backgrounds. The most serious offenders are housed at the Maximum Security facility, and are locked down for 23 hours a day. At the opposite end of the security continuum is the minimum security prison, which houses inmates for minor offenses and is referred to as a "work house" facility. In between are the Modular, Medium, and Occoquan facilities, with various levels of security and probably the most diverse group of offenders. These facilities house many inmates who have been moved down from maximum security. Finally, Lorton Correctional Complex contains a youth center which houses younger offenders, and which also houses most female offenders.

Gaining access to a facility at the Lorton Correctional Complex proved to be quite a difficult task, involving several weeks of correspondence (telephone conversations and letters) with D.C. Department of Corrections officials. After several preliminary conversations and interviews, I was given official permission from the Department of Corrections, Planning Analysis Division to conduct my study at the Central facility on March 24, 1994. At that time, I was given a Department of Corrections Order which establishes guidelines for the screening, control, monitoring, and conduct of research activities. I gained access also to the Occoquan facility through the Office of Religious and Volunteer Services. They agreed to allow me to accompany volunteer Mrs. Anne Knight on her weekly visits to that facility.

At Central, I was greeted by Ms. Brenda Makins, Programs Administrator, and Sgt. Woods, Training Coordinator. They conducted a thorough orientation which included a tour of the facility, a video-tape on contraband and an orientation package. I was introduced to several staff members there, including the Administrator of Central Facility, Mr. Vincent Gibbons. It was agreed that I would do research at the facility on Wednesdays and Fridays from 10:00 a.m. until 2:00 p.m. through the end of August. At that time, I was assigned to Mr. Robert Rix, Clinical Psychologist, who would be coordinating my research activities.

On entering Lorton prison, one is overwhelmed by the endless and all-encompassing effect of chain-linked fences and barbed wire. The guard in the front gate watch tower laughingly remarked to me "you'll have to stay now for at least five years" (Watch Tower Guard, Central). I was met by four officers at the Check Point. My impression of the procedures there was overshadowed by the gross negligence by which visitors and staff are "shaked down." Confusion over tasks, which book to sign in, and who will conduct the "search" procedure seemed to plague the staff there, diverting their attention away from the necessary precautions and accurate details needed to screen all those entering the prison. I was then escorted to the Administration Building where I was told to wait for Sgt. Sandra Woods, Training Coordinator.

Sgt. Woods was a very kind and friendly officer who gave me some valuable advice on how a female survives such an environment on a daily basis. "Everyday, you come in here naked...," she said (Sgt. Woods, Central). She told me to keep that in mind and never let down my guard when speaking to **anyone** at the facility, since [they] "get away with murder today" (Sgt. Woods, Central). Always stand with your back to a wall, she explained, and stay close to a door through which you can make a quick exit if necessary.

I then watched a video tape on contraband that lasted about 50 minutes. It described the various items by which inmates can and have in the past made assault and escape weapons. Knives are the most commonly made contraband items, and can be constructed out of kitchen utensils, glass, tweezers, toothbrushes, razors, metal sheets, and pens. Sgt. Woods also explained to me the various rules and regulations governing employees and volunteers of the D.C. Department of Corrections. After speaking with Sgt. Woods, I was taken on a tour of the facility by Ms. Brenda Makins, Programs Coordinator.

Lorton Central is a 68-acre compound about 25 miles south of Washington, D.C., located on farmland in Lorton, Virginia. Twenty-seven dormitories house an average of 1,350 long-term felons who have committed serious crimes in the District. Other buildings include the mess hall, infirmary, gymnasium, chapel, industries, diagnostics/new admissions, and control building. The outsides of the buildings are all made out of red brick, and look old, run-down, beat-up, dreary and depressing. There are no trees or gardens surrounding the complex; no windows to let the sun shine in the buildings; no voices of small children playing and laughing; no air-condition to alleviate the hot scorching days of summer; no cars to take a drive on a cool night in the fall...so many things are missing, things we take for granted on the outside, but learn to appreciate when we see life -or lack of life - without them.

Information provided by the D.C. Department of corrections indicates that Central Facility staffing authority consists of 438 Uniformed Professional Staff, and 141 Non-Uniformed Staff. The prison administration is over 90% black, with Correctional Staff consisting of 71% males and 29% females, and Non-Correctional Staff consisting of 65% males and 35% females. The inmate population is 98% black. 99.2% of inmates are convicted felons. The average years of incarceration is 7.7 and the average number of previous charges/arrests is 12. The average years of education of inmates is nine. Over 74% of the inmates at Central are between the ages of 18 and 39.

The Fiscal Year 1993 appropriated budget allocation for the Central Facility was $22,880,000 -personal services (salaries) $18,371,000 and non personal services (supplies, service contracts and equipment) $4,009,000. The

Fiscal Year 1994 appropriated budget allocation for the Central Facility is $21,549,000 -personal services $17,831,000 and non-personal services $3,718,000 (see figures 1.1-1.3).

Figure 1.1

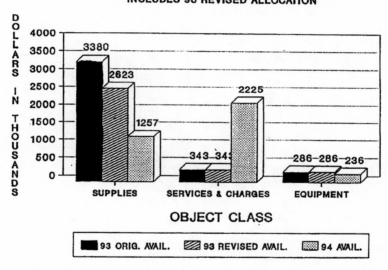

CENTRAL FACILITY'S BUDGET 93 - 94
INCLUDES 93 REVISED ALLOCATION

Figure 1.2

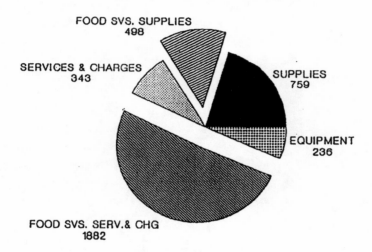

CENTRAL FACILITY'S 1994 BUDGET
FOOD SVS. FUNDING NOT ACCESSIBLE

FOOD SVS. SUPPLIES
498

SERVICES & CHARGES
343

SUPPLIES
759

EQUIPMENT
236

FOOD SVS. SERV.& CHG
1882

94 ALLOCATION INCLUDES FOOD SVS.

Figure 1.3

CENTRAL FACILITY'S BUDGET HISTORY

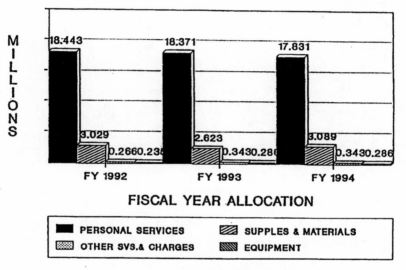

FISCAL YEAR ALLOCATION

51

Officially, according to literature provided by the D.C. department of corrections, various programs are offered to the resident population to "ensure that the quality of life is enhanced and that the programs are reflective of the identified needs of the population". With regard to academic education, the facility offers Adults Basic Education, GED prep and University of D.C. programs. The average participation in Academic programs (as percentage of average daily population) is 45%.

Vocational training programs are offered in the following fields: auto mechanics, barbering, plumbing, dental technology, carpentry, culinary arts, electricity, printing, graphic arts, dry wall, digital electronics, building maintenance, auto body, and brick masonry. The average participation in vocational programs (as percentage of average daily population) is 23%.

There are a variety of industrial and non-industrial work details. Salaries and enrollment vary according to assignment. There are an average of 100 resident inmates in each of the work-shops, and the average salary is $45 per month. Work details include the garment, metal, print, furniture repair and industrial shops; and dormitory, laundry and culinary squads. The shops include work assignments for the institution itself (grass cutting, furniture, uniforms, food, etc.) and for the D.C. Government (Signs, paper-work, furniture, uniforms, etc.) The estimated production of the industrial shops for F.Y. 1994 was 7.6 million (D.C. Govt., Dept. of Analysis).

The Psychological Services Center provides all of the psychological services for all residents at the Central Facility. The Psychologists and Social Workers are responsible for many tasks involving the welfare of the residents. The following is a list of the services provided by the Psychological Center:

> group and individual counseling
> psychological evaluations
> crisis intervention counseling
> self-help groups
> reclassifications boards
> forensic referrals

substance abuse referrals
mental health observations
psychotropic medication treatment
community resources and case management

Religious services seek to provide an equitable program of religious education that would provide opportunities for spiritual growth to all interested residents of the facility. It is believed that religious programs and activities are a vital portion of the rehabilitation process. The following activities and services are available to the resident population:

Islamic Activities
Jewish Activities
Bible Studies
Catholic Services
Protestant Worship Services

There are five Islamic communities in the facility. The Muslim resident population makes up 48% of those who attend religious services. Recreational opportunities are offered to the residents of Central Facility in six basic areas: intra- mural activities, varsity level activities, sedentary activities, free play, arts and crafts, and extra-mural program. Activities include:

vollyball
softball
pool
table games (cards, chess)
boxing
hobby crafts (ceramics, art, wood work, etc)
ping pong
flagball
soccer
tackle football
running clubs
music appreciation (band, singing groups, choir)

The following organizations exist with the assistance of community members, staff, and inmates:

alcoholics anonymous
narcotics anonymous
people animals love
NAACP
Healthy Eaters Connection
Lifers
Youth Movement Group
Concerned Fathers
UDC Prison College Program
ALNA House (Adults Learning New Alternative
Family Literacy Program

CHAPTER 4: INSIDE LORTON CENTRAL: THE PRISON REGIME

Central Facility is operated under a "unit management concept," as a way of supervision for the resident population. This concept consists of the breaking down of the larger resident population into smaller, more manageable groups. Unit staff members are placed in close proximity to the residents which in theory establishes better relationships and improves the delivery of services. The unit management staff consists of one unit manager, 2 or 3 case managers, one staff psychologist, 2 or 3 correctional officers and one secretary.

The D.C. Department of Corrections has identified eight essential ingredients for the overall success of the unit management approach. Leadership includes the central office, institution, and unit levels; a commitment at each level is seen as imperative to successful implementation. Secondly, each unit must have a written plan/mission which is specific and clearly defines its purpose. Moreover, the institution has to provide what is necessary to carry out the unit's mission. Competent staff is regarded as essential, where competency skills should include a commitment and personal resolve to the principals of unit management. Quality performance is an element which is directly related to the skill level of unit staff and is essential to a fully effective process. Successful unit management requires interdivisional cooperation between the various correctional disciplines. Another essential ingredient, monitoring and evaluation, states that a systematic approach to the evaluation of unit management is necessary to determine if its goals have been attained. Finally, analysis and refinement are essential whereby outcome needs are to be evaluated and analyzed with a view towards refinement of activities, programs and efforts to maximize overall effectiveness and efficiency.

The D.C. Department has also outlined six major objectives of unit management. These are the **stated** goals of the institution with regard to its basic operations and procedures:

(1)   to divide large numbers of inmates into well-defined groups, whose members are encouraged to develop a common identity and close association with each other and with unit staff.

(2)   to increase the frequency of contacts and the quality of relationships between staff and inmates by placing decision making personnel in proximity to those inmates assigned to the unit.

(3)   to provide better observation of inmates, thereby enabling early detection of problems before they reach critical proportions.

(4)   to improve inmate accountability and control by holding inmates accountable for their own self-control and actions.

(5)   to provide differential program strategies/interventions for each inmate depending upon his/her needs, abilities and ambitions.

(6) to place special emphasis upon the following:

- institutional adjustment
- work skill acquisition
- interpersonal communications
- positive self-esteem
- self-motivation
- problem solving techniques
- realistic goal setting
- education and training
- other life skill acquisitions

We can glean several important details from the above mentioned administrative and institutional goals of Central Facility, as a medium security prison. The two major components of institutionalization have come to revolve around two main components: custody and treatment. The custodial aspect of prison life forms the basis of the routines and activities upon which rests the foundations of staff and inmate relations.

Security within Central begins in and is coordinated by the command center. The command center is a room with thousands of lights, cameras, televisions screens, buttons and switches that are somehow all manipulated and operated to maintain a continuous surveillance over the movement within and around the institution. Operations run round the clock to ensure the maintenance of security and the provision of orderly control of the resident population. There are three shifts designed to accomplish the custody goal of the institution: number one shift (11:30 p.m. - 8:00 a.m.), number two shift (7:30 a.m. - 4:00 p.m.), and number three shift (3:30 p.m. - 12:00 midnight). The security force at Central also consists of 10 watch towers, each manned with an armed officer, twenty-four hours a day.

Besides custody, there exists another equally important ingredient or aspect of the institutional regime, namely, treatment. The facility treatment component is composed of a multi-disciplinary team of staff who expose residents to all avenues for rehabilitation. This is an attempt to turn residents into productive law abiding citizens who can function properly in the community.

There are no provisions which outline the steps necessary for the administration to take in order to ensure that official rules and regulations are met according to the stated objectives, concepts and ideological approaches. For now, I do not wish to comment on the above mentioned observations, but merely to point to their existence as facts to be later questioned, investigated and hopefully answered. With this information in mind, it is necessary now to turn to that aspect of the prison regime known as "intake.

> ...the indignity begins from the moment you walk through the gate...strip searches, body cavity searches...from then on you're just another number...(Inmate Central).

Intake can be seen as both a process of entry and exit. The inmate is entering a whole new world of convict life and identity and at the same time is exiting or leaving behind another life - a life filled with old friends, family, co-workers, social ties and community activities - a life which must now become only a faint memory of the past and a flickering hope of the future. For the time being, however, the inmate must go through several steps, phases and procedures that are all a part of the intake process.

Admission to Central prison is precluded by an intake screening and assessment for the mental health of the individual resident. This screening is to be conducted by qualified health care personnel prior to the placement of the resident in the general population or a housing unit. Screening includes inquiry into past history and present treatment of mental disturbance, suicidal tendencies, and hospitalization history, as well as observation of current mental state, appearance, conduct and behavior (D.C. Department of Corrections). A needs assessment/evaluation is also conducted for each inmate in the following areas:

> health/medical
> psychological
> substance abuse
> vocational
> educational
> social/personal skills
> work assignment

Upon entry into the institution, residents must go through a process of orientation about the rules, guidelines and procedures of Central. They are informed about dining procedures, mail, visiting, telephone privileges, authorized property and disciplinary procedures. Residents are given several forms to sign, indicating that they have been properly informed of all the necessary orientation steps. Inmates are then issued an identification card with a D.C. Department of Corrections Number, given institutional clothing, and assigned to a dormitory and work squad; and this is when the true process of "orientation" to prison life begins. Figure 2 summarizes the admissions process to Central:

Figure 2

ADMISSION TO CENTRAL FACILITY: FLOW CHART

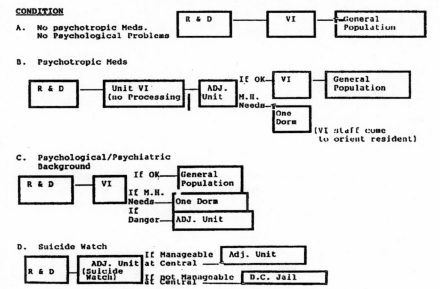

CONDITION

A. No psychotropic Meds.
    No Psychological Problems

R & D — VI — General Population

B. Psychotropic Meds

R & D — Unit VI (no Processing) — ADJ. Unit

If OK — VI — General Population

M.H.
Needs — One Dorm

(VI staff come to orient resident)

C. Psychological/Psychiatric Background

R & D — VI

If OK — General Population

If M.H.
Needs — One Dorm

If Danger — ADJ. Unit

D. Suicide Watch

R & D — ADJ. Unit (Suicide Watch)

If Manageable at Central — Adj. Unit

If not Manageable at Central — D.C. Jail

59

Upon entry into prison, inmates are deprived of their personal possessions, stripped of their former identities and re-socialized for prison life, being placed under the absolute control of a hierarchy of officials (Trestar, 1981). This process is very similar to what Goffman describes at being a key aspect of entrance into "total institutions" (Goffman, 1961). This further dehumanizes inmates as they lose their adulthood by being placed in a situation of forced childhood, having no control over their time or actions. The prison is a miniature society, with its own system of stratification, culture, language, roles and means of accommodating to the power differential between the "rulers" and the "ruled" (Trestar, 1981).

In essence, the prison becomes a social world which the individual inmate comes to adopt, whereby he/she cannot survive outside the institution (Goffman, 1961; Sykes, 1958). This notion becomes painfully and obviously clear from the following story described to me by the head clerk in the Records Department at Central:

> ...time is a big thing here at Central; there was a man whose sentence was up and he had to leave. He came to me crying and said he wasn't ready to go. I told him hey man your time is up, you have to go. He said to me, 'Mr. S---if I punch you in the mouth, I would have to stay, right?' Before I finished saying yes, the man swung his arm and "POW" hit me right in the lip! I shook my head a little and with all my nerve swung my arm and "POW" I hit him right in the mouth. I looked at him and said, 'now we're even,' you're still leaving... (Clerk, Records Dept., Central).

Prison life is characterized by routine and monotony, as daily activity is strictly regimented (Sykes, 1958). A typical day in the life of an inmate consists of:

5:00 am	wake-up/count time
6:00	count clear/breakfast
7:00	shift change/count time
8:00	day shift comes to work (administrative and treatment staff) work details for 8-4 work lines
9:00 - 10:30	morning yard-for inmates who do not work
10:30 - 11:30	return to cell - count
11:30	count clear/lunch
12:30 pm	return to cell
1:00 - 2:30	afternoon yard - for inmates who did not go to morning yard
2:30	return to cell

3:00	shift change
4:00	afternoon count
5:00	count clear
6:00 - 8:30	even recreation - gymnasium, phone calls, programs
9:00	lock down
11:30	count time/midnight shift
12:00 am	count clear
1:00	count
2:00	count
3:00	count
4:00	count
5:00	another day

Thus, while inside the walls of the prison, the life and behavior of the inmate is characterized by a routine which is constant and monotonous. Within this context, the inmate becomes easily susceptible to regression, apathy and listlessness, as everything has been done for him and to him, and in this primitive, infantile state, he can no longer make decisions on his own (Trestar, 1981). Therefore, upon entry into prison, inmates must learn the new rules and expected roles in their new setting as the old way of doing things becomes irrelevant to say the least and at most is totally forgotten.

In the sections to come, we will examine and investigate this new setting and describe the unique ways of thinking and behaving it produces. We will attempt to understand the dynamics of modern prison life by identifying the various social forces affecting prison organization today and how these phenomena have come to shape its course of operation and interaction among prisoners and staff.

CHAPTER 5: THE REALITIES OF PRISON LIFE: AN EXAMINATION OF THE DATA

The Inmate Social World: Inmate-Inmate Relations

...'Mel' had 2 bottles of gin per week and a supply of valium...that's how he did his time...
(Inmate, Central).

The concept of "doing time" in prison revolves around fulfilling the various needs that arise from the many deprivations and often horrid conditions that inmates must deal with upon entry into prison, similar to what Sykes refers to as the "pains of imprisonment" (Sykes, 1958). In 1983, a government inspection of Lorton Central Prison found numerous deficiencies, code violations and health hazards in the infirmary, kitchen, cafeteria, culinary shop, canteen, industries building, work shops, gymnasium, control room and dormitories of the facility. The inspection was prompted by a class action suit brought against the D.C. Department of Corrections by the law firm of Covington and Burling on the behalf of Lorton inmates. The case, termed the "12 John Does," was responsible for making several changes in the management and operation of Central Prison. Ironically, however, complaints, violations of health standards, hazardous and faulty equipment and in general deficiencies in several areas of living continue to exist on a wide scale level throughout the facility. Despite the much abhorred and oft complained about conditions at Central, residents there told me that the most profound loss an inmate faces is the loss of liberty. The confinement of the individual represents a complete rejection of him by society (Sykes, 1958; Irwin, 1970; Trestar, 1981). The blue uniform I saw them wearing day in and day out, the six digit identification number, the constant subordination to officials and most of all the years, months, days and hours that he has to serve, are all constant reminders that the prisoner is isolated from the rest of society. A clerk at the records department recalls a story about an inmate's reaction to his loss of liberty:

> a man once made a complaint to us (records) that his sentence was computed wrong and wanted us to re-do it... we did it and told him that we certainly did find out that there was a mistake in his sentence...he owed the department 1,052 days...he died that same night of a heart attack...he wasn't that old...i'll never forget that man...never... (Clerk, Records Dept., Central).

Doing time in prison also means the deprivation of many material goods and services that are a basic part of daily living. Control and possession of one's material environment is a strong indicator of man's personal worth. (Sykes, 1958; Irwin 1970). However, in prison, inmates explained, "the government owns the inmate," - his clothes, his tooth brush, his comb, his bed, his sheets, the pillow he sleeps on, the phone he uses, and every article, equipment, and facility he uses to live, breathe, function and exist inside the prison walls. Even those few items that he can call his "own" are not really his; an inmate explains:

> nothing is really your own in prison...even if it **belongs** to you; if it comes to giving a "bully" your sports magazine or being jumped while brushing your teeth at night...well...what would you do (Inmate, Central).

While it is true that the prisoner's basic material needs are met - he does not go hungry, he is allowed to exercise, and he is given medical attention - the fact that these standards of living are so regimented as to when, where, what type and how much, is a symbolic reflection of the inmate's loss of personal worth, self identity and autonomy, what Goffman calls "mortification" (Goffman, 1961). The endless lines at the mess hall, the rigid hours of the infirmary and the dozens of men standing in the hot sun waiting for the officer to open the gym at the precise hour, are all inevitable marks of forced childhood, engraved upon the inmate's mental image of himself, his character, and his being. This image creates a pronounced sense of deprivation, as Goffman notes, which echoes a marked anger, frustration and hostility against the institutional provision of inmate needs.

The following incident which took place at the infirmary brings to light the essence of the inmate's sense of deprivation. An inmate came in one afternoon at about 1:15 to the infirmary complaining of severe stomach cramps. He stood behind a sort of chain linked fence with an automatic lock steel door that closed off the infirmary from the inmate waiting area. The officer at the desk, without even looking up, told the inmate to come back at 1:30 when sick call began. Despite the inmate's urgent pleas for a doctor and his moans of pain and anguish, the officer remained unmoved, uncaring, and expressionless. Finally, the inmate turned around, still holding his stomach, and yelled as he left the infirmary, "this is neglect, this is genocide...they're trying to kill us all...they need to shut this whole fucking place down...just burn it up" (Inmate, Central).

The inmates at Central also expressed a strong sense of injustice with regard to the meals that they are being served. The Court appointed dietician at Central informed me that the meals there are "devoid of nutritional value and prepared in unsanitary kitchens" (Dietician, Central). Hot meals are served in the summer and cold sandwiches in the winter. Sometimes, preparation of food takes long hours due to faulty and old equipment, causing the rapid growth of bacteria in the food. An inmate explained to me the grumbling about the meals as an effort on the part of the inmates to be treated like human beings; "I know we broke the law," he said, "but we're still human beings, not animals" (Inmate, Central).

Besides material goods and services, inmates suffer from the forced deprivation of heterosexual relationships. Neither conjugal visits nor sexually explicit material are allowed at Central and strict rules and regulations govern the visits of an inmate's wife, girlfriend or mistress to avoid any sexual overtones. Forced to rely on memory, mental imagery and fantasy, an inmate must either suppress his sexual drive or engage in homosexual relations. More often than not, however, homosexuality within the prison institution is an act of violence and

64

aggression whose perpetrators impose upon younger, weaker inmates (Scacco, 1975; Lockwood, 1980). More will be said about these activities in later sections of the study. For now, it is sufficient to underscore the prevalent frustrations arising from the deprivation of heterosexual relationships, as an inmate's manhood - his masculinity - is constantly being questioned and attacked under the urgent need of heightened physical desire.

The dominant value system operating among the inmate population in the modern prison is that of suspicion, hostility and predatory behavior. A psychologist comments,

> the values we know - being kind, caring, responsive, do not exist inside prison walls - here, [you] try to get as much as you can without giving back and be as hostile as you can and get away with it...suspicion exists at various levels - inmates of inmates, inmates of guards, guards of inmates, and guards of guards... (Staff Psychologist, Central).

The element of suspicion arises from and is compounded by the carrying on of illegal activities, and the fear of who will cover for who and who will not cover at all. These illegal activities have come to dominate all aspects of inmate social life and are based upon a complex and extensive sub rosa economic system that is intertwined with clique and gang activity (Irwin, 1980). All inmates become involved to a certain extent and in varying degrees in the many different forms of inmate contraband economics:

(1) Food

A large portion of the inmate "underground" economy revolves around feeding. The first time I spent the day at the mess hall I was told by the Lieutenant there that they weren't punching meal tickets today. When I asked him why not, he commented, "this meal is so bad, no one will try to come for seconds" (Lieutenant, Central). Meals at Central are prepared by the inmates assigned to the culinary work squad. Preparation of food takes place in the kitchen of the mess hall. Conditions for the preparation of meals there are far from being ideal and quite short from being sanitary. During my many visits there, the temperature in the Cafeteria was always above ninety degrees. On several occasions, dish-washing machines were broken down and dishes were being cleaned manually with cold water. At one time, the drains in the kitchen floor were stopped up and a deadening stench was radiating into the kitchen and out to the dining area. I found out later that the odor was coming from dead cats that had fallen into the drains. The nutritional quality of the meals served there are far below governmental standards and guidelines, as described and explained by a court appointed dietician at Central. "I would never eat this shit," she commented (Dietician, Central).

Inmates are constantly complaining about the food at Central. As I was sitting one day during lunch at a table with a group of inmates, eating an ice-cream sandwich, an inmate came up to me and put out his hand. His palm was filled with grease, apparently from holding the grilled cheese sandwich that was being served that day. Not knowing who I am but assuming I was some type of important official, he looked at me and with a low, somber voice and his hands all greasy, asked, "will you please help us?"

Thus, it is easy to see how food can quickly become an item in the contraband system. Contraband food items originate primarily from the mess hall. It is contraband essentially because it is not allowed outside of the mess hall and into the dormitories. According to the rules of the institution, the only food items allowed in the dormitories are those from the canteen -coffee, tea, canned beans, tuna, fruits, etc. However, these items tend to be expensive for most inmates and therefore, alternative sources are sought.

The items stolen from the canteen are endless and can be anything from a bologna sandwich and potato chips to milk, eggs and butter, to coffee and tea. Inmates told me that these items are ordinarily smuggled by individuals who have kitchen duties and can gain easy access to supplies. Alot of times they sell it directly to individual inmates in the compound in exchange for other goods and services - telephone privileges, access to a typewriter, cigarettes, extra towels from the laundry squad, toiletries and a host of other items. Some individuals, however, give these items to their friends and members of their cliques who either keep it for themselves, or in turn sell it to others. An inmate recalled to me the following story:

> every Friday evening we'd go visit "Squeaky" in -- Dormitory out on the Northwalk...i'm not sure why they called him squeaky, but they did...man, it was like hanging out at the grocery store...he had everything - fresh fruits, sugar, milk, cheese, sandwiches...I mean everything, and if you wanted something he didn't have he would get it for you (Inmate, Central).

"Squeaky" was not operating the market alone. I learned from close friends of his that he was a member of an elite gang of street hustlers who operated and ran a "whole lot of other different contraband systems." More will be said about their activities in later sections. Although this food operation was referred to by inmates as "small scale" "jive" and "punk", I still wondered how on earth it was possible to keep that "grocery store" well supplied all the time. When I asked the residents who knew about "Squeaky's" how he got away with keeping all that food in the dorm they told me that the guards there got a "cut" of the profit.

Not all contraband food items are part of a profit seeking venture. Inmates use several techniques of creativity and innovation to create items that they are deprived from. Homemade alcohol or "shoots" as they call it is made out of anything and everything - apples, tomatoes, sugar, orange peel, and the like. An inmate described to me a most innovative and creative technique he and a group of his buddies used to make nachos:

> ...we were gonna watch a movie one night and we wanted to have nachos. We got some tortilla chips, slabs of velveeta cheese, olives and peppers that had all been ripped off from the mess hall...we threw all the ingredients in a garbage bag and put it in the dryer for ten minutes...we had some of the best nachos that night... (Inmate, Central).

(2) Sex

Illicit sexual activity occurs at various levels within the prison social system (Scacco, 1975; Lockwood, 1980; Bowker, 1980; Fleisher, 1987). The three major activities prevalent amongst the inmate population at Central are homosexuality, homosexual rape and voluntary sexual activity between inmates and female staff.

Homosexual relationships usually develop between inmates who were homosexual before their arrival to prison (Bowker, 1980). These individuals usually attempt to hide their affair from other inmates for fear of being poked fun at, assaulted or even killed (Bowker, 1980). Their encounters usually take place in the dormitories, bathrooms and laundry rooms, with someone who is a "trusted" third party being the "look out" man (Inmate, Central).

As in mainstream society, homosexuals in prison, once identified, become the objects of mistreatment and abuse (Irwin, 1980; Bowker, 1980). They are forced to do favors, cover for and sometimes even "take the rap" for the illegal activities of other inmates. However, as shown in the literature, these individuals often become targets of violence as they are preyed upon by aggressive inmates who have turned to homosexuality as a means of relieving their sexual frustrations (Scacco, 1975; Bowker, 1980; Lockwood, 1980; Braswell et al., 1985). Even young men who are not homosexual are often coerced, bribed or force to play the part of the female in the homosexual liaison. In such cases, sex is used as a means of power, violence, intimidation and revenge.

The fear of sexual assault is prevalent among inmates at Central. This fear is coupled with the anxiety over the AIDS virus, as 2 out of 30 inmates at Central are tested as HIV+. Sex pressuring, sexual harassment and rape are prevalent in the prison social setting, and continue to be a constant source of anxiety, fear, assault and homicide. This is consistent with the findings of Scacco, Lockwood, Bowker and other studies of prison sexual violence. I was told by the IGP (Inmate Grievance Procedure) Officer that incidents of sexual assaults happen "almost every day" and often occur in dormitories where they usually go unnoticed, undetected or ignored and overlooked by guards. A young inmate describes life in an environment where homosexual rape in an all male society is used as an

68

affirmation of masculinity:

> ...I had just come here and told myself I was gonna stay out of trouble...one day I was working when out of no where five men approached me; it took them less than a minute to get me on the floor and pull my pants down...they all did it, one by one, and I could hear the rest of them laughing and jeering. The act itself was scary of course...but it's realizing that it could happen again and again at any time, no matter where you are...that's what's really scary. And, I mean, what can you do? Throw a few punches, resist for awhile...if you're not damned scared by the surprise alone, there's always enough of them so that they'll do it...eventually anyhow (Inmate, Central).

Another form of illicit sexuality activity, not quite elaborated in the literature, are the voluntary sexual affairs that occur between inmates and female staff. This activity will be discussed in detail in the sections to follow on inmate-staff relations. Suffice it to say here that relations between inmates and female correctional officers have come to involve such activities as prostitution, exchange of favors, romantic interludes, long-term love affairs and even love triangles. These activities have resulted in the termination of several staff members at Central.

(3) Weapons

Frequent "shake downs," or searches of dormitories reveal that deadly weapons are widespread and easily accessible at Central. Knives or "shanks" are the most commonly used weapon for assault. These contraband items are obtained by the inmate through several means -they are bought, exchanged for other contraband goods, made by the individual himself and smuggled in by visitors or staff. "Almost everyone owns a shank," explained an inmate, "we have to protect ourselves somehow."

On a routine "shake down" or search of a dormitory, I accompanied a Sergeant into an inmate's room. The room was a mess - newspapers and magazines all over the place, empty boxes of food, cigarette butts, clothes, books, shoes and candy wrappers all made for a relatively disorganized, jumbled up disaster area. To me, the area looked like the product of an undisciplined teenager rebelling against his mother's ardent demands to keep his room clean and in order. However, the Sergeant told me that this was the work of a real pro. Sometimes, he explained, one of the guards tips the inmates off that there will be a shake down that afternoon. Inmates with something to hide then turn their rooms upside down so that it would be so messy that the officer doing the search wouldn't bother to look too closely. As the Sergeant was explaining this, he overturned a book and under it, he found a six inch screw driver sharpened into a deadly pointed shank. I was stunned at what had just happened. He explained to me that this happens all the time and that the individual was probably using it for protection purposes. He confiscated the weapon and began to write up a disciplinary report for the inmate to give to the Captain.

Although carried for protection, the shank is also used commonly for settling "beefs," or building up a violent reputation. Inmates explained that a young man entering prison for the first time might have to "knife" someone just to avoid being harassed and picked on by so called "bullies". More will be said about these acts of violence in later sections. The point here is that assault weapons are readily available in prison at any time and for anybody to use...but how and why is this so?

Weapons are made available at Central at various levels. The manufacturing of assault weapons is made possible via the access to sharp items from the industrial work shops and also the kitchen and infirmary. On my many visits to industries, there was never more than two or three officers supervising the 150 inmates working in the shops. They expressed a serious concern over the inmates' access to glass and metal and said that it was impossible to keep full track of all their behaviors during the hours that they are there. In the industrial shops, the inmates have access to metal, glass, plastic, nails, screw drivers and other sharp and potentially dangerous objects. While the inmates are searched and they do go through a metal detector when they leave the shop area, it is still quite possible to sneak some contraband items past the officer, as on several occasions, the metal detector was not working. Knives and shanks are also made from razor blades, sharpened pens, tweezers, typewriter letters, kitchen utensils and even sharpened tooth brushes. Brooms and mop handles are also used as clubs. These items circulate with ease among the inmates on the compound and are sharpened, manipulated and somehow shaped to become deadly weapons for stabbing and bashing.

More sophisticated weaponry such as hand guns and grenades haves been known to show up during random shakedowns. Investigations revealed that these items are brought in primarily by staff members who have some kind of connection to an inmate at the facility. Also, vendors supplying food products, raw materials, medical supplies and equipment, and other products to the facility are a major link in the availability of weapons. An officer emphatically expressed to me that "they [vendors] can bring in an entire arsenal that would blow up this whole damned joint..." (Corporal, Central). When I asked him how come, he recounted to me the following story:

> ...that [s.o.b.] in the watch tower in the back gate where all them trucks come in every day is a goddamn alcoholic. Once, a white shirt (Lieutenant) walking around the compound looked up and saw that there was no officer in that tower at the back gate post. He radioed to him but there was no answer. The gate was wide open and a medical supplies vendor was at the gate probably wondering what the hell was going on...later on the white shirt climbed up the tower to see what was going on...he found the officer on duty in the back gate watch tower passed out on the ground with a bottle of liquor next to him...**that's how come!** (Corporal, Central).

These dynamics will be investigated in further detail in the discussion of inmate-staff relations.

(4) The Rackets: Money, Loan-sharking, Gambling

Consistent with Irwin's observational development of importation theory (1980), an inmate describes prison as "a miniature town...an extension of the streets, where..the same things that a dude did on the outside, he can come in and do the same thing in prison" (Inmate, Central).

The exchange of money is strictly prohibited at Central. Individual inmates have accounts from which they can make legitimate purchases from the canteen or commissary, use the telephone, or buy stamps. The major medium of exchange in prison economics has long been cigarettes (Kalinich, 1980).

However, as Irwin notes, the expansion of the contraband system over the years has produced a supply and demand for goods, services and activities that are items of high price and value (Irwin, 1980). Thus, money lending and buying credit have become important aspects of the contraband system. Each walk has an individual who is operating a sophisticated money- lending business. He is usually referred to as a loan shark and can usually allow reliable individuals to purchase goods and services on credit. Loan sharks are also known to lend money to inmates to conduct drug transactions with contacts outside on the streets. The rate of return for purchasing credit or obtaining a loan is often 100% for regular customers but can be negotiated for a friend, buddy or as a favor. Loan-sharking is a risky business, but, as I found out from inmates actively involved in such transactions, the rate of return outweighs the cost of getting involved.

The credit system gives rise to the need for an external exchange system (Kalinich, 1980). Accordingly, most inmates have a bank account of their own outside the institution. Friends or relatives become involved and money transactions occur during visitations, through the mail, or through trusted guards. Inmates sometimes have relatives send them money which can be deposited directly into another inmate's institutional account or outside bank account (Kalinich, 1980). A large part of "hustling," as inmates call it, revolves around gambling activities. Gambling takes a variety of forms and sometimes even starts as friendly wagers between inmates. An inmate told me he and a group of residents once entered a bet as to how long it would take for this one officer with a certain "reputation" to become romantically involved with an inmate. When I asked him who won the bet, he said "we all did...that bitch got involved so quickly...well, we got a good old laugh out of it anyway; and that was sufficient payment" (Inmate, Central).

More serious gambling activities usually involve card, dice, or pool games, placing bets on horse races, sporting events, presidential elections, and the lottery. Professional bookies within the prison run the operation and consistently accept bets and payoffs from inmates (Kalinich, 1980). These activities can take place anywhere in the institution; contacts usually concentrate in the dining hall, chapel, dormitory, at work, or during a movie. Most inmates gamble as a preferred form of entertainment, especially when it comes to sporting events (Kalinich, 1980). Almost all inmates become involved in normative gambling activity on some level. However, large- scale gambling with dice and cards where huge sums of money are involved can and often do, as an inmate put it, "turn into risky, life-threatening incidents." Professional collectors exist to ensure that inmates repay their debts within thirty days or else they are instructed by the bookmaker to turn violent on the debtor or even threaten his family members on the outside. The whole system bears a striking resemblance to the illegal rackets that take place out on the streets. Here then is a society where many activities take place that are very similar to those activities that take place in our own society, but with slightly different rules, patterns and consequences. It is the various dynamics of social organization within the prison environment, however, that shape the course of activities and interactions among inmates. The process is illuminated brightly by understanding the dynamics of the most expansive illegitimate activity that occurs at central: drug trafficking.

(5) Drug Trafficking

"I am going to impose a sentence...recommend a federal
designation so that he won't be at Lorton. So that he won't have the drugs that are possible available to people so freely down there and available to him" (D.C. Superior Court Judge Henry Greene, Feb. 22, 1984, quoted in *The Washington Post*, Nov. 17, 1993, A22).

"There's a certain frustration with a law enforcement system that puts people into an institution where there's a major problem with drugs" (U.S. Attorney Helen F. Fahey, quoted in *The Washington Post*, Nov. 16, 1993, A16.

On November 15, 1993, U.S. District Judge T.S. Ellis III, refused to send a prisoner convicted of possessing drugs inside the Lorton Correctional Complex back to that prison stating emphatically that "the ease with which inmates can obtain drugs in Lorton is a public scandal " (Washington Post, Nov. 16, 1993: A14).

Federal investigations, shakedowns of prisoners, occasional dormitory sweeps, searches of visitors and my interviews with staff and inmates have all revealed the Lorton Correctional Complex as a place where drugs are widely available. Investigating officers told me that drugs are smuggled into the prison on commercial trucks delivering goods and supplies to the institution, by officers and professional staff, by volunteers, through the mail, by residents with access to the infirmary, and most commonly by visitors. Materials, supplies and equipment to feed, clothe and house the 1,500 or so residents at Central that are hauled in every day through the back gate create a great deal of traffic there. Guards posted at that gate told me that they are primarily concerned about escapes and therefore, trucks and other vehicles coming in and out of the facility are not and cannot realistically be thoroughly searched for contraband. A lieutenant investigating staff corruption told me that front gate officers are also "paid off by drug smugglers to avoid being searched thoroughly."

Exchanges between visitors and residents can occur rather easily. Drugs are smuggled in various items such as a baby diaper, sanitary napkin, orally and under parts of the visitor's clothing or inside the visitor's body cavities. A lieutenant vividly recounted to me a sting operation conducted in the visiting room on an inmate who was suspected through information given by an informant, of smuggling drugs into the institution:

> there are seven officers in the visiting room watching between 75-100 inmates and visitors. Usually they can get away with doing anything during visits...even have sex. Yeah, you better believe it. But that day, we were all watching him and his lady friend. We witnessed the whole thing, because another inmate who's a snitch told us to watch him. About ten minutes into the visit, we saw the lady put one leg on the inmate's lap. She then unzipped her pants and stuck her hand down her pants and started pulling at something. We could see the inmate tell her 'hurry up god damn it, pull it out, pull the damn stuff out. She kept reaching down her pants and we could see her struggling. Finally, the inmate forcefully stuck his hand down her pants and pulled out the drugs...and he must of really stuck his hand all the way up her vaginal canal because we heard her give a muffled shreak of agonizing pain. As soon as the drugs were in his hands, our officers moved in on him. He tried to react quickly and swallow the drugs but we cuffed him after wrestling him onto the floor...he really put up a good fight. His lady

74

friend was arrested too and sent to the D.C. Jail...she really gonna be in alot of trouble because she'll be charged with possession with intent to distribute. She brought in with her 30 small bags of heroin...can you believe that, thirty bags! That ass was about to swallow thirty bags of heroin, and for what? A fifty dollar profit, a hundred dollar profit? Man it just ain't worth it. (inmates are strip searched after visitation and therefore, they smuggle the drugs in by swallowing them and later on passing them) (Lieutenant, Central).

I was told by several informants that a great deal of prison violence is related to drug trafficking - a deal gone bad, somebody does not deliver, the goods are not what was promised - an argument occurs, fights break out and the violence escalates. An inmate told me that "beefs" surrounding drug deals can result in the most violent confrontations. "It's a matter of trust and respect," he said, "...even in prison, a deal's a deal...and if your ass ain't covered, you're dead" (Inmate, Central). Although drug trafficking is a well known phenomenon at Central, the specific deals and transactions are kept under a tight system of silence. Some residents refused to talk to me at all about the drug activities; when I asked them why not they emphatically stated, "because it's illegal!" What they did tell me however, is the necessary code of silence that exists when it comes to dealing drugs. "You don't mess up when it comes to drugs," an inmate told me, "there's a prescription for death if you don't keep your mouth shut" (Inmate, Central).

Any type of drug is readily available in the inmate economy, as found by Kalinich (1980) - PCP, heroin, marijuana, amphetamines, tranquilizers and cocaine. The highly addictive love boat (PCP) or "boat" as the inmates call it is the most popular drug among the inmates. It produces hallucinations, delusions and flash backs that make the inmate feel both paranoid and powerful. He feels that everybody is out to get him but no one can overcome him. An officer describes an inmate who was "tripping":

...he was totally outraged...we couldn't understand why at that time, but everyone knew to stay out of his way; he was attacking anybody and everybody. Four or five officers were trying to hold him down and he still put up a good fight...he was ready to do anything, even kill somebody...and believe me, the way he was acting, he sure could of (Officer, Central).

Marijuana "joints" are also very popular. One of the "finer" pleasures of prison life, as one inmate put it, is playing poker on a Saturday evening and getting high on a joint.

The supply of drugs is kept at a steady flow. Several factors facilitate this operation. The major reason behind the readily available drug market is simply the inability of the administration to exert sufficient control over the operation of the facility and over the inmate population (Sykes, 1958; Irwin, 1980; Colvin, 1993). The size of the facility, the inmate to guard ratio in the dormitories (about 25 to 1) and the relative mobility of the residents all create problems of control which to a large extent facilitate the flow of contraband. Moreover, the structure of the institution allows for free interaction between inmates who tend to congregate in areas that are basically unsupervised or poorly supervised (Irwin, 1980). Thus, inmates can easily and secretly make drug transactions in the mess hall, during films, in the gym during recreation, in the yard, in the dormitories, at group therapy sessions, at AA meetings, and even in the line at the commissary or canteen. This is further compounded by the fact that a large number of officers and staff members, including case managers, counselors and psychologists, are actively involved in the drug trafficking industry (Lieutenant, Central). Security is also lax at the check point. Staff, officers, visitors, lawyers, court officials and other guests are patted down by an officer and go through a metal detector. I spent several hours at the check-point observing the interactions between the staff and individuals entering the institution. There is always a heavy flow of traffic with people coming in and out of the facility, paperwork being filled out, phones being answered, and radios being operated to inform certain locations in the compound of incoming visitors. On several occasions, I observed staff members who are well known and long time volunteers at the facility slipping by security, and entering into the facility without being searched. Moreover, the patting down of individuals is a very inefficient search method, and the following experiment I conducted vividly illustrates this point:

it was towards the end of my research, so I figured it would be worth taking the risk. I thought to myself, what's the worse that could happen? They could temporarily detain me, strip search me, ask me to leave and worse of all, terminate my research there. But I figured it wouldn't be that bad...after all, it's only baking soda!! So I did it. One morning, I took one ziplock bag and filled it, oh, about half-way with crystal clear, high quality, perfectly cut white stuff --baking soda that is. I taped the bag to my stomach and wore my usual dress shirt and pants with low heeled shoes and panty hose. I arrived at the check point at Central at exactly 10:00 and tried to act as normal as possible. I signed in the green visitor's log book as usual and put down my note book and lunch bag to be searched. After that, I went through the metal detector which beeped as usual because of my keys in my pocket. Then came the scarry part. The female officer approached me as usual to conduct the "shake down." I tried my best to hide my fear, tension and anxiety. I don't think she detected any change in me. Her hands went down my sides, down my chest to the middle of my stomach and down my legs...then it happened...she walked away, as usual, as always when I have nothing at all on my body, except this time, I was carrying several ounces of --- baking soda (see figure 3):

Figure 3

Smuggling Drugs Into Central Prison: An Experiment

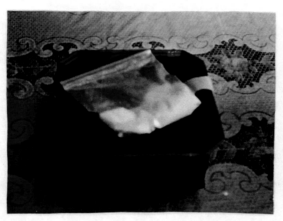

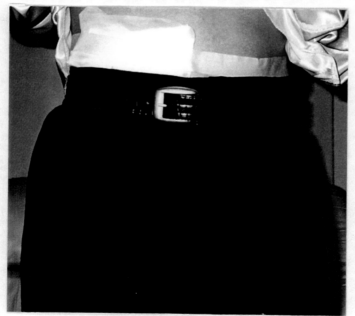

Thus, it is clear to see the ease with which drugs can flow inside the prison. However, contraband drugs can be obtained from within the facility itself. Some amphetamines and tranquilizers are stolen from the prison infirmary by inmates with work details in the pharmacy and sold through the inmate contraband economy (Infirmary Staff, Central). On occasion, residents with legal prescriptions sell some of their pills to other residents for a monetary profit or exchange them for services. By and large though, drug-trafficking is an enormous operation that revolves around the smuggling in of illegal drugs from the streets. Information given to me by both staff and inmates indicates that the biggest motive to get involved in drug trafficking in prison is profit. The price of drugs in prison is anywhere from 2 to 3 times higher than on the streets, yielding a profit margin that is high enough to make it well worth the risk. Inmates working in prison make very trivial amounts of money, ranging from $12 a month to $100 a month. This is usually insufficient to purchase luxury items from the commissary and there is therefore an incentive to get involved in the contraband economic system, with drug trafficking being the most profitable racket. Also, a great deal of inmates send the money they make from drug transactions home to their needy families. Some inmates become involved in the drug trafficking to support a drug addiction. These individuals are referred to as "crack heads" and "speed freaks." While some inmates at Central get drug treatment therapy through the various rehabilitation programs, the accessibility and availability of drugs makes the temptation too great for many other addicts. Finally, some inmates become involved in the drug market simply for the thrill and "bad" reputation, what an inmate described as "living the fast life and making quick money."

The dynamics of organization of the modern prison, with the vast expansion of the contraband economic system and other rule breaking activities, has given rise to several roles to accommodate the informal organization of inmate activities within the prison setting. This is consistent with the underlying assumptions of Sykes' deprivation model (Sykes, 1958). An inmate described the informal social organization of inmate activities in the following way:

> ...prison is an extension of the free society...we have our own rules, our own way of doing things, and we know when to do them and who does what. Things usually run smoothly...as long as everybody cooperates in the roles they take or are seen to play; some situations arise, but in a close, hostile environment, your way of dealing with the situation is different...it has to be, the rules are different (Inmate, Central).

Through my many conversations, interviews, observations, interaction in staff and inmate activities, and the close bond of trust and friendship that developed between me and some of the inmates at Central, I discovered a world of social roles and interactions that revolve primarily on the successful operation of illegal activities. Some of these roles reflect the behavioral and personality characteristics of the inmates that play them. Others are simply the product of the special prison argot assigned to individuals who perform certain activities. Whatever the case, the various roles adopted in prison develop to accommodate some type of position in the informal social organization of inmate relations and activities (Sykes, 1958; Irwin, 1970, 1980). Several roles emerge within the prison setting to accommodate and facilitate the distribution of money and contraband. In previous studies (Sykes, 1958; Cressey, 1961; Clemmer, 1958) the distribution of contraband is described as being controlled by a few individuals (merchants and politicians) who had a monopoly over prison commodities. These individuals were usually abhorred but tolerated by other inmates as part of the convict social system. The "politicians" and "merchants" usually had a great deal of power as they had control over scarce goods and services and had some influence over the administration. However, with the vast expansion of illegal goods smuggled in from the outside, prison gangs came to dominate the contraband system and replace individual entrepreneurs with groups of racketeers who sell as well as rob other prisoners.

Gangs or "cliques" as they are referred to, are organized around various legal and illegal activities. This phenomenon is well established in the works of Jacobs (1977) and Irwin (1980), where gangs are described as penetrating the everyday aspects of prison life (Jacobs, 1977). Some well known groups that "hang" together are the "Jamaican brothers", the "school nerds" (individuals in academic programs), the "vocational training buddies," Muslim groups such as the Moors and Nation of Islam and the "street hustlers." The clique serves as a means of identification, status, resource and protection for the individual inmate. He feels that there is someone he can turn to if a problem arises, someone to share his worries and concerns, someone to provide support and leadership. This is parallel to what Jacobs describes as the important function of "psychological support" that a gang can provide to the inmate (Jacobs, 1977). An inmate described to me his feelings of loyalty to his clique:

> how far you'll go with each other makes you a clique or gang; would you slash someone for me, take the wrap for me, cover my ass on a debt...that sort of thing. I would do anything for my buddies...even die. You can't be considered part of the gang if you're not willing to do that. I love those people...man, they do anything for me...they hooked me up with the right people, built me a good rep [reputation] took care of some tight beefs I had with a couple of guys; they're like brothers, real brothers. I hated life...prison life, but now, I have a group of people that I can call my people...they're the only ones that give a damn about me in this joint; they're my family (Inmate, Central).

Leadership roles are of vital importance to preserve the integrity of the specific activities, rules and guidelines of the gangs (Irwin, 1980). Leaders have several characteristics, with charismatic authority being a sort of prerequisite to the role. Leaders have to have the ability to enforce codes and rules which are all part of an informal system of control. Accordingly, they are usually inmates who have an extensive and broad knowledge of the informal institutional structure of the inmate social system from past experience in prison. They are also usually individuals who still have a long way to go before they are released or are eligible to come before the parole board. Moreover, leaders have work details that allow them to move about freely within the compound, and can gain access to dormitories, industrial shops, and other buildings with relative ease. Leaders also have to have contact with a large number of fellow inmates who work with them and for them, as well as a vast knowledge of criminals on the outside who facilitate their activities in prison by providing resources in terms of goods, drugs and money, to help fund and develop their operations. Leaders must establish good relations with both inmates and staff, and must give both sides the illusion of trust and stability. Thus, it is their duty and within their best interest to maintain the status quo within the inmate social organization through the use of overt and covert tactics of force, coercion, and manipulation to establish order and control.

Specialized roles must emerge to cope with the vast array of illegal activities within the prison, when money, street money or "green" as the prisoners call it, becomes imperative in running the rackets (Irwin, 1980). A "sugar-daddy" is an individual who operates a money racket, and his activities go well beyond that of the "merchant" described by Sykes, who simply sells what he really should give (Sykes, 1958). The sugar-daddy is usually a street hustler who continues his conning activities behind bars. Like the merchant, the sugar-daddy is not well liked by other inmates who see him as preying upon the miseries of the vulnerable; however, he is trusted to some extent regarding money transactions. Sugar-daddies usually build "good" relations with certain guards who most likely know about their operations and even on occasion borrow money from them when they are involved in illegal activities and transactions with inmates. They also need to build a certain type of reputation among the inmate population - a sort of respect that emanates from a fear. Sugar-daddies are often inmates with an expansive knowledge of the informal social organization of the prison. They also must have a large supply of cash or "bank" available to run their business, usually money accumulated within the prison or from the outside. Accordingly, they are individuals who have done alot of time and or are facing alot of time ahead of them. Thus, they have nothing to lose and therefore, will resort to any means to command respect and instill fear. The sugar-daddy tries to "play it cool" all the time, like a gangster whose quiet presence is enough to produce tension and anxiety to anyone who crosses his path; however, his role is marked by ruthless, cold acts of manipulation, coercion, violence and the-preying upon of individuals who are weak and desperate.

Big time drug traffickers are referred to as "major dealers." These individuals control the base operation of drug trafficking and distribution in prison. The most necessary and crucial characteristic of major dealers is that they have an extensive knowledge of drug trafficking from off the streets. They must know major drug dealers on the street whom they can trust to help nourish their prison operations through constant supply of "clean" goods. They often have the reputation of being tough gang leaders and big time drug dealers on the streets and this reputation extends to them in prison. They usually have contact with those inmates with work details that can facilitate the smuggling of drugs into the facility and accommodate its circulation throughout the compound. Major dealers must also have small time dealers working for them to make contacts with specific buyers. However, it is the major dealer who takes the risk of soliciting the help of guards and other corrupt staff in the operation of their drug organizations. Major dealers typically have a great deal of time to serve and therefore, take the risk of running such a racket to better their status in prison. Major dealers do indeed have a higher status in prison - better clothes, food, luxury items such as t.v.'s, radios, and walk-mans, and of course more money to buy illegal goods and services. In a way, the major dealer resembles a modern version of Sykes' "real man," who is seen by the inmates as the prison hero who is able to pull his own time (Sykes, 1958). But, unlike the real man, he exploits other inmates in his drug dealings. Thus, the major dealer, the new prison hero is looked up to by young inmates who admire him for his flashy lifestyle, and not for his ability to maintain integrity in the face of deprivation (Sykes, 1958). Although tough, heartless, and ruthless, an inmate describes how he feels about a major dealer he works for:

> ...man, what can I say, I love the dude...he's bad, I mean he so bad ain't nothing get to him. He's sort of my idol; I wanna be just like him, a big time dealer with lots of clothes, money and of course women...you should see the way females be all over him, just because they know he's a fast guy. ...I really admire him because he's tough and he don't take no shit from anyone...not even the officers; especially not the officers. That's the reputation I want for my self, because...well, that's the type of person I am, a real bad dude (Inmate, Central).

Big time drug trafficking operations in the prison also create the need for specialized individuals to smuggle drugs in while eluding the authorities. Accordingly, individuals, referred to in a somewhat humorous manner by inmates as "slam dunkers," are experts in storing balloons full of narcotics deep enough in their anal cavities to be hidden from view in the mandatory strip search conducted as they exit the visiting room. The covert world of the slam dunker was revealed to me by an inmate who has adopted this role for the past three years. Slam dunkers are often younger inmates with contacts to major drug dealers on the streets, inmates with a history of drug offenses and who are trying to live the "fast" life. They usually have their wives or girl friends smuggle the drugs into the visiting room for them. Often, slam dunkers will swallow the balloon of narcotics, depending upon its size. Thus, these individuals are the basic keys to the drug trafficking industry, as their role represents the major means of successfully smuggling drugs into the institution vis a vis their visitors, of course. Slam dunkers sometimes work on their own and run their own drug operations. However, they usually work for a major drug dealer and get a cut of the profits. Since their role is critical, they are individuals who are trusted by the dealer to deliver the goods as promised. Sometimes, a greedy slam dunker will try to outsmart the dealer by keeping the goods to sell himself. However, as my informant put it, "this is a deadly game that very few play and even fewer get away with." It is often the slam dunkers who fall prey to an inmate who snitches to authorities about a drug trafficking operation, which makes their roles especially risky.

The role of the "snitch" has taken on new meaning in the modern prison social organization. The term snitching or "ratting" has always been reserved in previous prison literature for those individuals who buddy up to the authorities by squealing on certain illegal activities that some inmates participate in -gambling, stealing food from the mess hall, making illegal phone calls, carrying a weapon, and attacking another inmate (Sykes, 1958; Irwin, 1970). However, recently, with the expansive drug operations and transactions that occur behind prison walls, snitches often take the role of informants by "ratting" on other inmates involved in drug trafficking (Lieutenant, Central). Usually "snitches" are forced or coerced into playing this role due to being caught with drugs, either on them or during a shakedown of a dormitory. Snitches are not big time drug dealers and often are even drug addicts who have drugs to support their habits and not to distribute. They are not part of any major drug operation and accordingly have few contacts or buddies who can get them out of a jam. Thus, they can sell out by turning to the authorities and informing them how and from whom they get their supply of drugs. These type of snitches, if known, are considered "marked for dead" and therefore must be placed in protective custody and eventually transferred to another institution for their own protection. Snitching is generally looked down upon by inmates as the most despicable act an inmate can do. Accordingly, individuals **suspected** of being snitches are "roughed" up a little to avoid any future problems they might create. An inmate describes what happened to an inmate who was thought to be a snitch:

> ...we snuck up on him as he was walking back to his dorm from the mess hall. There were about four of us, and we jumped him. He kept saying, 'man you have the wrong guy, man you have the wrong guy,' but we wanted to make sure he got the message...just in case; and that kind of thing goes around fast too (Inmate, Central).

"Punks" are individuals who are described by inmates as "kissing ass" or "buddying up too much" to the authorities not for purposes of snitching but for their own benefit. They abide by all the rules of the institution even if they hate them or disagree with them secretly and actually despise the authorities. These individuals sometimes make friends with certain guards, but they are treated suspiciously by both staff and other inmates because of their passivity and acquiescence. This role is compatible to what Sykes calls the "center man," who comes to adopt the beliefs and attitudes of the authorities, with a "slavish submission" (Sykes, 1958). An officer commented, "there's no way that 'punk' is going straight...he must be up to something; I just don't trust this turning over a new leaf act...". Alot of times, they do special favors for staff such as clean their offices, type something for them or do their paper work. In return, the staff members grant them certain requests such as assignment to a specific dormitory or work detail. When I asked a group of younger inmates what they thought of going to school, earning a degree, learning a trade, being polite to authority and generally acting according to institutional rules and guidelines, they responded, "man...that's punk," "that ain't cool," "that's not fly." The role of the punk is thus reserved to those inmates who are almost **always** involved in "good" institutional activities such as educational and vocational programs, group therapy sessions, church events and the like. These inmates seemed to always look "neat" - they always wear their clothes properly, shirt tucked in, ironed pants - as opposed to the other inmates whose pants are hanging halfway down their hips, their shoes untied and all scuffed up. Their beds are always made and their rooms kept clean. The predominant characteristic of these individuals is that they are usually young, with relatively short sentences and they do not really ever become immersed in the convict culture and identity. It is these individuals that always said to me, "I don't really belong here," or "I'm different than these other guys here." Even though they are not completely on the side of the staff, they are seen by most inmates as being "sell outs" and "butt kissers." Despite their negative reputation, punks are generally left alone by other inmates and never really become involved in any major illegal activities or fall prey to random or non-random acts of violence, unless they have some kind of beef with another inmate.

"Loners" are inmates who have very little contact with other inmates or with staff members. Like punks, they are individuals with short sentences. However, they are older inmates who have gone in and out of prison over many years and are just tired of being part of the system. Loners try to stay away from cliques, from the contraband system and other illegal activities, from trading favors, and generally from becoming involved in any behaviors which may stir up trouble. These individuals are sometimes referred to by the younger inmates as "old timers" or "pops." They are often sought out by other inmates for advice in tough situations and even occasionally arbitrate between two inmates in settling a dispute. Loners are well respected by the inmate population and are generally seen as being peacemakers by the staff. A loner described to me his present status:

> ...I've been in and out of that gate too many times, and this is my last time. I have 7 more months to go...that's why I don't talk to nobody or get involved in nobody's business; you get to learn to hold your own ground, be silent at times and know when to speak. You never accept prison as a way of life...you just deal with it (Inmate, Central).

Discussing sex was not an easy task. Few inmates were willing to talk about their own sexual activities. However, sexual relations among the inmate population occur at various levels. The sexual patterns described to me by inmates did not seem to, as did with Sykes' typology of "wolves," "punks" and "fags," involve a break down of sexual roles according to who plays an active, aggressive role and who plays a more passive, "feminine" role (Sykes, 1958). However, there is a general agreement that those individuals who are openly or visibly homosexual are called, in the language of the inmates, "fags." These individuals were usually homosexuals on the streets who continue their activities in prison. However, there are individuals who become active homosexuals inside prison due to the deprivation of heterosexual relations (Sykes, 1958). An inmate who does not openly admit to being involved in homosexual activity describes the role of the fag:

> ...fags are considered to be our women. They're soft, well groomed, tight assed and, well, sex is sex. Some of them walk in here and before they even get off the bus, there be men hanging out the window staring them down, waiting at a shot at getting a piece of their ass. ...alot of men here love their partners like a wife...they protect them and keep them from messing around with other inmates... especially with AIDS and everything. Some of those bitches cost a fortune...just like an expensive lady; they want everything from you -drugs, alcohol and extra goodies; man, just like a goddamn expensive girlfriend (Inmate, Central).

Homosexuals have a very negative reputation among the inmate population. Homosexuals are seen as weak, disgusting, "sick," and not to be trusted. An inmate told me that next to snitches, homosexuals were regarded as the most disgusting and despicable inmates. They are constantly harassed, made fun of, and jeered at by other inmates. On a more serious level though, fags often become the targets of violence. As suggested by Lockwood, this type of homosexual gets into trouble with other inmates who may interpret his gestures as propositions or flirtations and become offended and defensive (Lockwood, 1980). An inmate explains:

> ...I wasn't about to let that fucking asshole think I was some goddamn fag, so I had to teach him a lesson in respect. A group of my buddies and me came up to him in the bathroom and jumped him. We almost killed the son of a bitch. We told him to keep his ass to himself and told him he was a fucking homo and we wondered if his momma knew what he was doing or if his poppa wouldn't kick his ass for doing the things he do...he never bothered me after that (Inmate Central).

It is quite clear that homosexuals have a very tough time in prison, and thus, inmates are very hesitant to admit to this behavior, let alone openly practice homosexuality. However, it is important to note that the role of the prison homosexual is reserved exclusively to those individuals who are openly homosexual and who readily admit to their activities. On a larger scale, homosexual acts are committed by a large number of individuals who turn to it as a sexual outlet due to frustration from the deprivation of heterosexual relations. These individuals tend to be violent, aggressive "bullies" who may prey upon younger inmates who are not homosexuals themselves. However, very few individuals were willing to discuss these types of relationships, for fear of retaliation.

Despite the agreement in general among inmates about different roles, there are no absolute values for certain types of roles and behaviors. Situations, times, and people change, alter, and develop to meet new demands and requirements. The discussion of the inmate social system would not be complete however without making a detailed investigation of the staff involvement in inmate activities and affairs. Until now, my observations have been purposely reserved to those incidences of inmate relations to one another. I wish to enter now the realm of inmate- staff relationships, to further expand the knowledge and understanding of the prison social organization.

The Captives v. The Captors: Inmate-Staff Relations

> Prison is best run by the residents...now that the administration has interfered too much with the inmate social system, it's much worse (Officer, Central).

The traditional view of a correctional officer attributes his authority to his or her ability to command respect and exercise discipline amongst the prison population (Carroll, 1974; Lombardo, 1981). The administration was feared because the inmates knew what measures would be taken if certain rules were violated. Interactions between guards and inmates were restricted to those activities and encounters proscribed by the official rules and guidelines. The lines were drawn separating the world of guards from the world of inmates, with very few exceptions to the rules. However, today, inmate-staff relations paint a completely different picture, a picture marked by the unusual shades and undertones of mutual suspicion, disrespect and distrust.

Crouch notes that,

> twenty-five years ago, prisons were politically and legally isolated from the societal mainstream. Officials frequently operated according to self determined and unquestioned policies which made guarding and doing time predictable, if not always constitutional. The subordinate status of prisoners was clearly defined, and role expectations were unequivocal. Officers maintained dominance over inmates by whatever means they found practical and were typically supported by their superiors. But as political, social and legal activists criticized prison conditions and operations, inmates gained power relative to their keepers (Crouch, 1991).

The key to inmate-staff relations in the modern correctional setting is the ability of correctional officers to manipulate the system of rewards and punishment to gain compliance from the inmates and therefore tip the scale of power in their favor (Sykes, 1958; Lombardo, 1981). There are no set rules, regulations or criteria that govern the interactions between officers and inmates. An inmate explained, "one day, a dude [officer] can write you up for wearing dark sunglasses and the next day, another dude will ask you to get him the same pair." The enforcement of rules governing inmate activities and behavior is inconsistent, arbitrary and marked by a rampant system of favoritism that usually works to the detriment of both officers and inmates. A Lieutenant describes the delicate balance of rewards

89

and punishments in a correctional setting:

> ...getting respect is not easy around here; you have officers that are total idiots. I had an inmate come to me one day and tell me that the officer on his walk wouldn't write him a pass to go to the infirmary. When I investigated what was going on, I found out the officer couldn't read or write. Now, you see, how the hell do you expect an inmate to have respect for that officer. He probably thinks to himself, 'man, you're no different than I am...you just as sorry and pitiful; you have the same standards and you just happening to be wearing a uniform.' So, because the line between officers and inmates is so blurred, the officers have to let the inmates think and know they have something they want or that they can give them something they don't want. It all boils down to pride. You scratch my back and i'll scratch yours. I tell an inmate to do something and he knows he has to do it or else I can lock him up, even if it's something small like stepping out of line at the mess hall or verbal abuse...especially verbal abuse. He knows I could either give him a little extra time with his hunny during visitation or I can send him to the hole for two weeks...if that doesn't break him, than I can send him back, for another two weeks, and...he'll break eventually...oh yeah, he'll break. and then i'll have his respect (Lieutenant, Central).

Officers often do favors for inmates that they like. This may include a dormitory transfer, change of work assignment, favorable reports and granting of furloughs. These favors are usually reciprocated by the inmate in many different ways, such as typing up a report for an officer or getting him/her an item from the inmate contraband economy. I was told by the head of the records department that Central has the unique feature of inmates and correctional officers coming from the same neighborhoods. Thus, many officers have previous friendships, associations and ties with inmates from the streets. They often hold the same values as the inmates and come from similar social and cultural backgrounds. The following exchange took place between a new officer touring the facility and an inmate in the print shop:

Inmate - (looking up from the task he was doing, distracted by the presence of visitors; he examines us closely and seems to recognize someone. He approaches us). Hey man, check you out...what's happening?
Officer - Alright, man, what's up with you? (Officer and inmate exchange a friendly handshake)
Inmate - How's the old neighborhood...them girls still looking so fine?
Officer - Yea, things still the same...anyway I have to go buddy; you take care of yourself and stay out of trouble.
Inmate - Alright man, it was good seeing you.

That officer later told me that the inmate in the print shop was an old friend of his from the neighborhood. They used to play ball together, go to school together, date girls together and even get into a little trouble together. "What a waste," he commented regretfully, "that guy is good people...my momma used to breast feed him and me together because his momma was always shooting up and never did pay any attention to him...man, we really do go back".

Often though, exchanges between inmates and staff can become quite hostile. Prison is a world where the precise rules are not clear and treatment of the inmates is often left to the whimsy of the officers (Crouch and Marquart, 1980; Fleisher, 1989; Haas and Alpert, 1991). Disciplinary actions are quite random and are not applied uniformly to all inmates. On several occasions, routine cell searches resulted in disciplinary reports against certain inmates for minor infractions. The same infractions stated in the reports were witnessed by me to be prevalent amongst many other inmates, against whom action was not taken.

Moreover, I met with an inmate who was locked up for 37 days in the hole, allegedly on 'suicide watch'. When I asked him what happened, he told me that the unit manager in his dormitory called him a "fucking homosexual" and that he became enraged and cursed back at her. "She had no right to say that to me," he said, "but I'm an inmate and she's staff, so I'm the one that was cuffed and put in the hole." Thus, a great deal of animosity exists between guards and inmates, which results in inmate violence directed at guards in the form of isolated instances of retaliation or in full scale prison riots (Braswell et al., 1985). The opposite is also true, as prison guards subject inmates to beatings in the name of order and discipline (Marquart, 1986). An officer at the infirmary described his feelings towards the inmates, with undertones of hatred and hostility. His comments were precipitated by an inmate's threatening to sue because he was in pain but couldn't see the doctor until 1:30:

> I grew up in some of the same neighborhoods as these people...but I made the right choices; i'm sympathetic but only to a certain extent...none of this foolishness. They come in here and as for medical attention, immediately...they don't even pay for it, it's not their right; you and I pay for it...alot. Sometimes they forget where they're at...you know what I mean? (Officer, Central).

The IGP (Inmate Grievance Procedure) Officer reported to me that inmates assault staff as frequent as staff assault inmates. He gets at least one complaint or report of an incident per day. "Stabbings occur all the time,"he explained, "inmates usually stab officers just simply because they don't like them." Most inmates harbor some strong anti-authority, anti-system sentiments. They feel the entire criminal justice system, and especially the prison system, is biased, unfair and cruel. Inmates express several concerns over being kept at the mercy of the guards who may and often do use unwarranted force on them, and who symbolize the unfair authority of the system itself (Marquart, 1986). Inmates also confirm the presence of what Bowker calls "psychological victimization" (Bowker, 1980).They report that on several occasions, guards will ignore the request of an inmate, hold an inmate's mail, destroy his property unnecessarily during a shakedown, threaten him with solitary confinement or the loss of parole status and even make up stories about his wife or girlfriend on the streets. Thus, many times, an inmate is just waiting for the opportunity to explode into violence, and usually, the object of his misery and frustrations is the officer in front of him. An inmate recounted to me the following story of an encounter turned violent between a lieutenant and an inmate:

> the inmate was called to the captain's office about a complaint a lieutenant had made about him. No one really knows or cares about what that beef was about, but everybody knew what happened after words. We all heard that --- was in the hole and the word traveled around that he had body slammed lieutenant ---, right in front of the captain, next to the warden's office...and that lieutenant is no small guy either. After the inmate body slammed him he told him 'I told you not to touch me.' That kind of stuff goes on all the time...I guess this incident was so famous because it involved a lieutenant, and a real big one too (Inmate, Central)

Clearly, correctional officers work in an extremely tense setting, with inmates out-numbering them by sometimes over 100 to 1 in a given location. Antagonisms between inmates and staff can develop over a period of time and may be taken to a very personal level. A Unit Manager expressed the following attitude about sex offenders:

> me and sexual offenders just don't get along...they should just lock em up

forever...they never change, no matter how much therapy they get (Unit Manager, Central).

Moreover, a great deal of officers view the inmates as convicted criminals deserving of punishment, and thus they react to many circumstances with abusive treatment and a general lack of respect (Lombardo, 1981). An older, respectable inmate was being harassed by an officer about using the telephone, when I saw the officer making him get off the phone by rudely and abruptly closing the line without notice and telling the inmate, "say good-bye". When he complained to his supervisor, he told him, "you're a convict and we're officers...do you expect us to respect you?" These hostile attitudes also extend to the property of inmates. On several shake-downs, I observed officers going through the personal property of inmates while making comments about family photographs, taking items such as slippers, candy and cigarettes, and unnecessarily destroying books and magazines.

On a more sophisticated level, the IGP investigator showed me several complaints of items reported missing by inmates such as tennis shoes, walk-mans, televisions and money. This confirms Bowker's finding of "economic victimization" of inmates by staff (Bowker, 1980). He showed me the results of a three month investigation into an inmate's complaint about his account being short $800. It turned out that an officer had stolen the money out of the inmate's account. Often, he said, an officer will purposely take something that belongs to an inmate he doesn't like, knowing that he would retaliate and eventually get sent to the hole. This type of hostile inmate-staff relation can become a personal vendetta and is heightened in the following encounter recounted to me by the lieutenant investigating the incident:

> We have an officer here that put a hit on an inmate...got him stabbed. What happened was one of our lady officers here apparently had a reputation amongst the inmates of being sort of loose...of having sex with the inmates. An inmate told her this and warned her that she better be careful because this kind of talk spreads easily and might reach the wrong people. She told him it was none of his goddamn business and that if he didn't shut his mouth that she would get him. That same week, that inmates was stabbed real bad. We talked to him in the infirmary and he wouldn't say much. We got most of our information from other witnesses. A week later, we discovered the officer's telephone number in another inmate's belongings. We think he's the one who may have carried out

the hit...who knows. One thing though, this sort of behavior will not be tolerated, especially from a uniformed officer...she's disgusting, real disgusting (Lieutenant, Central).

The above incident represents the intense and often deadly struggle for power that arises in the daily interactions between inmates and officers. The officer feels threatened by the inmate who may use the information he has against her to blackmail her. She must assert herself as the inmate's superior, despite her illegal activities. She must appear to be in control, she must portray herself as being in a position to make the inmates' lives easy or make them difficult. Likewise, the inmate tries to establish himself a reputation, create a sense of dignity and build self-esteem. He feels he has rights, and that despite the many injustices of the system, he can use these rights to his advantage. They try to manipulate the officers and use their weaknesses to their benefit. Indeed, the struggles continue and power is at the hands of whom ever can exploit their position to make the life of the other difficult enough to where he would become weaker. And at that point where the dynamics of social control reach a level of heightened social disorganization, there comes into light the famous Parsonian question over the problem of order (Parsons in Mayhew, 1982).

In a world where the bounds of the relations between inmates and staff are crossed indefinitely, achieving order within an environment of hostility, violence, and a general disregard for the rules and deep animosity towards the authorities, is very difficult if not impossible. Given the economic constraints on availability of adequate prison staff and the dynamics of prison organization, there arises the need for a less than total dominance of inmates by administrative staff and guards (Trestar, 1981). Prison organization is marked by a systematic attitude of tolerance, where rule violations regarded as minor or non- threatening are seen as an exchange for overall social order (Sykes, 1958; Trestar, 1981; Lombardo, 1981; Colvin, 1992). It is important to note that there are many different levels of tolerance and thus, each situation is evaluated according to the severity of its consequences.

Officers are evaluated, promoted and given pay increases based on the behavior of inmates in their charge. A sergeant explains:

> I became a sergeant real fast because I have a good rep amongst the white shirts [Lieutenants and Captains] because I run a good operation for them. There are some people that have been here twice as long as I have and still haven't moved up...you can move, yes, but you have to know what makes the administration happy: compliance and the **appearance** of order. That's it. As long as everything is running smoothly...no major law suits, no riots, no burning down administration buildings like a couple of years ago. That's order, and how we get it is by being diplomatic. You always have to remember that there are a whole lot more of them than us. So, I give a little, I take a little. I give alot, I expect alot. That's how it works, give and take...it's those officers that take too much without giving that never get anywhere; I guess they just never learn (Sergeant, Central).

Thus, as noted by Sykes (1958), realizing the relative impossibility of enforcing all rules due to the shortage in staff and due to the fact that inmates are not going to obey all the rules because of loyalty to their own organization, the custodians are willing to overlook many inmate infractions provided that inmates comply with the more important rules (Trestar, 1981). Officers are acutely aware force alone is inadequate to stop the inmates from collective acts of violence such as flooding dormitory bathrooms, burning down buildings and purposely destroying equipment and machinery. They are also aware that the system of rewards and punishments is insufficient to attract or induce inmates to conform to institutional regulations on the assumption of receiving benefits (Sykes, 1958; Trestar, 1981). Faced with the reality of their limitations, the individual officer frequently fails to report infractions that occur in his or her own presence. The officer sees an inmate smuggling food from the kitchen and turns the other way. The officer knows an inmate is running a money racket and pleads ignorance. The officer learns of a brutal plan to attack an inmate and purposely lets the incident take its course. The officer even transmits forbidden information to inmates such as shakedowns of certain dormitories.

Officers discover that by ignoring certain offenses, there is a meaningful trade-off with the inmate population in terms of over-all complacency and compliance (Trestar, 1981; Lombardo, 1981; Colvin, 1992). The officer cannot play "tough guy" all the time, for he is faced with inevitable disobedience, harassment, and even violent retaliation. He finds that it is best to claim the norm of reciprocity by overlooking certain illegal activities. In return, he will gain the assistance and cooperation of inmates in the satisfactory performance of his duties. Dormitories will be kept clean, clothes will be neatly worn, counts will be cleared with ease, work duties will be carried out with precision and reports of infractions will be kept to a minimum, all of which work together to make the officer appear to the administration to be running a smooth, tight, clean operation. The officer now appears to be worthy of a favorable evaluation due to his or her ability and capability to well manage and handle the population under his control. Therefore, the relationship between officer and inmate takes on the character of ongoing negotiations regarding decisions to take certain actions.

Failing to enforce all the rules all the time does not mean that inmates do not face negative sanctions for certain activities. The officer must evaluate the situation according to its consequences or its impact on the overall social order that he has established. Most officers know the inmates don't respect them as individuals neither do they regard their positions as legitimate authority to be obeyed. They simply see compliance as part of the system of rewards and punishments that usually works to the advantage of both officer and inmate (Lombardo, 1981; Trestar, 1981; Colvin, 1992). However, certain rule violations that bring negative sanctions often revolve around a personal encounter between an officer and an inmate. In such cases, the officer sees the need to play the authoritarian role, as the threat to his pride may cause a severe breakdown in the system of reciprocity and therefore he would lose his ground. An officer explains this situation:

> the count was taking an unusually long time to clear and this one guy needed to use the bathroom. I told him to wait a few minutes that count would be cleared soon. He asked me again and I told him to wait again. He then said 'fuck you hack' and pulled his pants down and peed in the trash can. He knew I would have to clean it up and he knew I would be humiliated. I couldn't let him do that. This was no minor violation because it involved my pride, and when it comes to pride it's either me or him, and I wasn't about to

96

let him get away with it. So I had him locked up for violation of count procedures, even though what he did wasn't a security threat...but it was a threat to my security because I would lose the 'respect' of the other inmates who saw what happened. That guy could have done anything else and I would of let it go, but this is different, this had to be taken care of. They have to know their limits...that certain things won't be tolerated. If they forget who they are then they'll walk all over you, and pretty soon, none of them will do anything for you...and it can't work that way, not in an environment where the people you deal with that you're supposed to keep in line will be there in your face tomorrow, the next day, the next week, the next month, the next year and probably till you leave the whole goddamn institution (Officer, Central).

The dynamics of organization within the prison setting indeed calls for the close proximity between the officers and the inmates (Sykes, 1958). The officer cannot withdraw from the world of the inmate, for he is intertwined in his behaviors and activities on a daily basis. This proximity of interaction often leads to the close and intimate association of prisoners with staff and, as Crouch and Marquart note, brings to light a more complex level of tolerance for rule violation and a reluctance to enforce all the rules: the actual participation of officers in inmate illegal activities (Crouch and Marquart, 1989). I wish to turn now to this underground world of interaction which bridges the gap between the captive and the captor.

Inmates do not see their custodians as correctional officers, viewing the idea of rehabilitation as a "real joke" since most of the staff are ridden with problems and need rehabilitation themselves. An inmate expresses a common sentiment and attitude:

how the hell can these hacks rehabilitate us when they got a whole load of problems themselves. How can they tell us not to use drugs when most of them would even fail a urine analysis. You tell me what I can learn from an officer who can't read or write when I have a college education. They hire a bunch of idiots and expect us to respect them and follow their example. There are alot of intelligent people here and they know better than that. We know these hacks come from the same neighborhoods as we do and they face the same problems as we do...that's why it's so easy for an officer to become a screw (Inmate, Central).

This attitude breeds a general apathy on the part of the inmates towards the officers. The inmate does not fear his position of authority nor is he impressed by or intimidated by the differential power structure between him and the officer. He knows that the administration's symbols of power are in reality afraid of the inmates. Unarmed, outnumbered and intimidated, the officer becomes the essence of vulnerability, conned and manipulated by the inmate to join him in his covert enterprises and illegal activities. This is not the only scenario however. For, on the flip side, as well documented in the findings of Crouch (1991), the officer, knowing he can exploit the inmate because of his unchecked ability and capacity to inconsistently and arbitrarily enforce the institutional rules, consciously or subconsciously, on purpose or accidentally, he chooses to betray his role as an officer of the law and instead joins the inmate in his underground pursuit of the same illegal activities he carried on out on the streets. There are various levels of staff violation of the rules and I wish to discuss these levels within the context of the specific roles an officer adopts and the activities he or she becomes a part of in their interaction with the inmates.

Inmates refer to correctional officers who are involved in small scale rule violations as "screw ups." These officers are usually relatively new on the compound and have the least amount of social distance from the inmates. Accordingly, they are often assigned to work shifts in the dormitories, the gym, the mess hall and other places of congregation where there is close interaction with large groups of inmates. New officers coming into the prison setting are usually unfamiliar with the informal rules of social organization by which the prison runs and operates on a day to day basis, and therefore they appear to be confused, hesitant and unsure. Thus, in such case, they often find themselves in some serious tight spots due to their over-zealous attitude and false sense of security and ambiance. An officer explained to me his experiences:

> I started off here as a real fire-ball. I wanted to run the whole damn place on my own. I thought I was real tough and that I could handle anything. My first day here...and those inmates were staring me down real good, as if they were trying to tell me something, to intimidate me; that made me angry. After all, I was the officer and they were supposed to be afraid of me...not in the sense of fear but in the sense of respect and authority. I tried to carry myself so that they would respect, so I picked on everyone and everything. I thought by building a reputation of taking no shit from nobody, this would make them be afraid of me. Then one day, an old timer [inmate] pulled me aside and said, 'hey brother, lighten up, are you trying to get yourself done?' I didn't take him too seriously until a senior officer told me the same thing. He said that I better stop acting so tough, that if an inmate don't like me, he can have me stabbed or killed. I figured I would take their

advice...it just isn't worth it, it isn't worth getting killed. It's enough that after a year of playing it hard with the inmates, I lost twenty-five pounds and began to take blood pressure medication...now you see me dealing with the system as any other person deals with his job. As long as nobody escapes on my shift i've done my duty; any of that rehabilitation...corrections ...that shit, I don't do that no more. I just try to pacify the inmates here...whatever it takes (Officer, Central).

Inmates explained that they can easily detect the uncertainty and confusion experienced by new officers on the beat, as they are "easy to sucker." Thus, they take advantage of their vulnerability and attempt to befriend them. The inmate acts polite and respectful to the officer. He is courteous and shows a genuine desire to obey the rules and perform his duties with accuracy and diligence. He even volunteers to help the officer in carrying out some of his tasks such as typing up reports, tidying up his office, doing some paperwork and filing, and organizing activities. Soon, the officer will begin to discuss his personal life with the inmate. He will tell him about what he did last weekend and what are some of his favorite hobbies. They will laugh about and bet on football games and other sports. He will talk about his wife and his kids. He will discuss some of the problems he is having with other staff members and ask the inmate for advice, and all the time, his trust for the inmate will increase.

After gaining this trust, the inmate begins a process of what is called "tripping with the officer," and getting him "right where [we] want him." Pretty soon, the inmate will discover a few of the officer's weaknesses - he may be short on money to pay the rent, he may have a drinking problem and he may even be using drugs. The inmate then begins to manipulate the officer to turn him against the administration and explains to him the many injustices that occur in some of the top offices. He lets the officer feel exploited by the system and portrays his role as insignificant, "puppet-like" and a mere symbol of the inhumanity of society. The officer begins to adopt these sentiments and looks to the inmate for support and encouragement. The inmate, describing the situation as "having the officer in the palm of [my] hand," now feels he can move in on him and take the next step of "exposing and attracting him to some of [our] underground world of vices." The inmate is confident that he has successfully placed the officer in the position whereby he is asking for means of making some quick cash. The inmate must be careful though, for he must make an accurate distinction between the officer who is a screw up and the officer who is a big time racketeer.

The screw up will only become involved in illegal activities to the extent that he will cover for an inmate in exchange for some favor or benefit in return. They are usually well aware of drug transactions and make sure that they are on duty when major transactions are taking place. They are sometimes cut a profit for acting as a middle man in making some drug deals. These types of officers will also inform inmates about surprise shakedowns of dormitories, about sting operations to be conducted by the administration and also, they will act as informants to inmates about which other inmates are snitching to the authorities. Screw ups will also conduct shakedowns of dormitories and confiscate certain contraband items. Instead of making a report and getting an inmate into trouble, they will keep the items for their own, as the inmate usually says, "hey man, that ain't mine, it's yours." They often receive cash, food items, radios, walk- mans and institutional favors from inmates in exchange for their 'troubles,' and generally are free from being harassed by the inmates.

Often, an inmate will prey upon an officer until he no longer needs him and then he will tell him to go find another means of making some money, that he no longer needs his services. He tells the officer

> ...man, you a sorry nobody, a srew up. You better not open your mouth or i'll go straight to the administration and tell them about your illegal activities. I have witnesses, you know, even other officers. They'll love getting rid of you...you a disgrace. You supposed to be an officer and do what you supposed to. At least i'm an inmate, i'm expected to screw up, what the hell is your excuse (Inmate, Central).

The officer begins to feel trapped by the inmate. He has no legal or administrative recourse to take against the inmate. He fears losing his job and losing his life. Feeling threatened, he sees the need to reassert himself and his status. He begins to communicate with other inmates and attempts to, as an inmate put it, "find out some dirt" on the inmate who betrayed him - who are his enemies, what beefs other inmates seem to have with him, etc. He then tries to make the life of that inmate a living hell. He steals some of his belongings, moves him down the ranks in dormitory status and work assignment, sets him up with a false beef, puts him at odds with other inmates, and generally attempts to retaliate against the inmate. The inmate at first does not suspect or get wind of what is going on, but, "nothing ever stays quiet in prison," explained inmates. Pretty soon, he finds out through the grape vine that "officer so and so has it in for him." He then bands with some of his inmate friends and even one or two trusted officers who do some work for him. He begins his own series of retaliations and the vicious circle of violence, and rule violation continues.

During my first two days at Central, I was surprised to see the number of female officers that are assigned to dormitory work shifts. The first time I heard the word "freak" was during a staff picnic which I attended. The picnic was intended to raise funds for the institution and was held in front of the administration building. They had hamburgers, hotdogs, fish sandwiches, sodas and snow cones. Uniformed staff were dressed in jeans and t-shirts and everyone seemed to be relaxed and having a good time and a few laughs. A few inmates assigned to work duties there were hanging around, bringing out extension cords, hooking up machines and participating casually by interacting with some of the staff in a very superficial, somewhat ostentatious manner. I admittedly began to eavesdrop on the conversations of people when my attention was caught by the words of one inmate to another, as their talk and manners resembled those of two highschool boys at their first freshman dance.

They were commenting about all the female staff at the picnic. I was guessing that it was somewhat interesting and exciting for them to see the female officers out of their uniforms, kind of like in high school when you see your raggedy classmates all dressed up at the school dance like real ladies. But there was more to their conversation than that. They were talking about the female officers, not just commenting about how they looked but about their relationships with men -with inmates. They were discussing who is going with who, who broke up with who and who's having who's baby. That's when I heard one of them commenting, "...yeah man, I know, she's a real freak." I found the courage to go up to them and say, "I'm sorry, I couldn't help over-hearing your conversation...but what on earth is a 'freak'?" The two inmates began to laugh and after looking at each other and nodding in what seemed to be approval to talk, proceeded to reveal to me a world of love triangles, jealousies, gossip and sex that went beyond my wildest expectations of interaction between officers and inmates.

I was told that a "freak" is a female officer who is having a sexual relation with an inmate or with many inmates. "There is so much sex going on around here between female officers and inmates," they elaborated, "some freaks move from inmate to inmate like prostitutes." I wondered what would make the officer take the risk of getting involved with an inmate when the streets are full of men looking to become romantically involved with a woman. However, when I began to understand the way the officers are manipulated by the inmates, I could see how such a relationship could evolve and develop. There are several reasons why a female officer might enter into a relationship with an inmate. She walks through the gates of the institution and past the administration building onto the walk where she is assigned to her work shift. All along the way, she hears comments from inmates, "hey beautiful," "hey gorgeous," "is that you bringing all that sunshine in," "why don't you share some of what you got with others," and so on. Now regardless of what she may look like, the officer begins to enjoy such praise and compliments. I learned through my conversations and interviews with inmates, staff and informants that many female officers come from poor neighborhoods and miserable relationships. They have been mistreated, abused and neglected. This sudden burst of attention brings them the unusual sense of feeling pretty, of being feminine and wanted or desirable which in turn builds up their self- esteem.

The inmates are well aware of these emotions. After all, they come from the same neighborhoods as these officers and they consequently know how women are treated there. They take advantage of the vulnerability of some of the female officers and begin to create the perfect scenario to begin a sexual relationship. But how can this be? How can the female officer fall into such a trap? "Very easily," a lieutenant emphatically told me, "we have some of the best cons here."

Love relationships between female officers and inmates begin in a very unsuspecting and "innocent" manner. Inmates pick and choose which women to prey upon. After all, they must be careful not to move in on the wrong officer for this can mean imminent disaster. Word travels fast on the prison compound. It seems like a small neighborhood where people know each other and where, as an inmate put it, "everybody knows the scoop on every one else's momma." Inmates and officers communicate information to one another and consequently, an inmate can get enough information on an officer to know her background - where she comes from, who she "goes with," what tough experiences, rejections and heart breaks she's had, if any, her weaknesses such as alcohol, money and drugs, and any other information which may lend the officer vulnerable to the inmate's charms and vices.

Knowing this information, the inmate begins to move in on his unsuspecting victim. He acts very polite and charming, with a "good morning mam," and a "good afternoon mam." He cleans her office, polishes the floor and takes out her trash. He does some typing for her and does her filing. All along, he seems to be innocently trying to turn a new leaf and attempts to do so by abiding by the rules and even becoming actively involved in some of the programs and meetings run by the officer. The officer notices this unusual attitude and takes a special interest in the inmate. She begins to verbally praise him and tell other inmates they should try to act like inmate so and so. The inmate picks up on this and sees it as being the catalyst for the beginning of his patterns of behaviors and activities leading up to a sexual relation with the officer. The following scenario was portrayed to me by a lieutenant who says he sees it happening all the time as the female officers "fall into the trap of the inmate," and enter into an illicit, dangerous affair:

> after some type of superficial, friendly relationship is established between the officer and the inmate, it can begin with something as simple as a pat on the shoulder when saying 'good morning.' The officer does not suspect a thing. She should tell the inmate to back off, and that he shouldn't be touching her. But she doesn't, she stays silent and by doing this, she gives the inmate the go ahead to move to the next level. The officer is having a problem with her computer and the inmate offers to help. He hovers over her shoulder and looks on to the screen with her. He does this for several minutes while playing with the keys on the keyboard until he finally fixes the problem. All along, the officer does not seem to be bothered by this invasion of personal space. Once again, she is giving the same message to the inmate, to further get closer to her. Now remember, these acts don't happen all of a sudden and too frequent...of course the inmate doesn't want to spook the officer or scare her away. It may take several weeks or even months...but they don't care, they've got alot of time. The next step is to become involved in the personal life of the officer. He finds out that she went to some concert last weekend and it just so happens that the group playing is also his favorite group. He brings her some tapes and they listen to the music together. He finds out who she went to the concert with, whether she has a boyfriend, a husband or children. He knows where she lives and they begin to reminisce about the old neighborhood. They talk about some of the wild night clubs there and turn out to know some of the same people. The inmate then begins to appear vulnerable, weak and far from the tough Lorton convict personality. He talks of how much he misses being back on the streets and how badly he wants to change. He creates this romanticized image of himself getting an honest job, going to church, becoming involved in community activities, getting help for his problems and having a good family. The officer sees this as genuine sincerity and begins to see the human side of the inmate. She feels that his attitude is ten times better than that of some of the men she knows on the streets. By now, the inmate feels comfortable enough to sit right next to the officer on the couch and the space between them has become smaller and smaller. She looks into his eyes intensely and he looks into her eyes. The inmate reads her expression very carefully. He knows she's fallen for him so he gets closer to her face. He starts to kiss her gently and sees she doesn't resist. He whispers sweet things in her ears just before taking the final steps towards removing her clothes...and by now I think you must have a pretty clear picture of what's gonna happen next (Lieutenant, Central).

Love relationships between female officers and inmates occur at various levels. Some affairs are just a one time thing while others can last for several months or even years. Some officers even become pregnant with an inmate's baby. Love triangles often develop and can become quite complicated and some female officers have even been transferred to other institutions because they were fighting with another officer over an inmate; "it's disgusting...just like a goddamn soap opera," commented an officer. Inmates admit that the officer in the relationship is usually the loser in the end, for in most cases, the inmate is simply using her to get some favors and privileges in return or, as some inmates put it, "to get some action." Inmates often enter relationships with female officers to get them to smuggle in drugs and thus, they become a major source for their drug trafficking operations. Once they get what they want from the officer, however, they end the relationship as if nothing had happened and no promises of love and faithfulness are ever kept. The officer feels threatened and vulnerable. She cannot retaliate and she cannot complain. An officer commented, "....they are left with broken hearts, broken promises and broken dreams...and I don't mean inmates either." Here than are real emotions and real feelings existing in relationships all over the world between men and women...even those behind bars, at a prison, where those type of feelings are supposedly strictly forbidden. But the strictly forbidden is seldom an inhibition for the emergence and development of the activity, and this will become painfully apparent in the section to follow on racketeering.

On November 17, 1993, *The Washington Post* reported that Federal authorities charged 17 current and former D.C. Corrections Department employees with taking bribes and helping to supply a long-flourishing drug trade inside the Lorton Correctional Complex (*The Washington Post,* November 17, 1993). On February 4, 1994, three former D.C. Corrections Department employees were sentenced to prison terms for taking bribes and helping to supply the drug trade in the Lorton Correctional Complex (*The Washington Post,* February 5, 1994). On April 1, 1994, a staff psychologist at the Lorton prison plead guilty to smuggling marijuana into the facility, and investigators said she had teamed with an inmate to sell drugs at the prison complex. (*The Washington Post*, April 2, 1994). By April 4, 1994, fifty-five prison employees had been arrested for smuggling drugs to inmates over a two year time period (*The Washington Post,* April 4, 1994).

The availability of drugs as a contraband item has become quite common in the modern prison (Fleisher, 1989; Fong and Buentello, 1991; Colvin, 1992). Information gathered through the intensive interviews of both staff and inmates indicate that a number of guards and professional staff at Central are actively involved in the smuggling and trafficking of drugs inside the prison. Although many personnel have been apprehended by various FBI sting operations, staff continue to become involved in the flow of drugs to inmates. My close interaction with staff revealed to me that a major motivating factor in the involvement of staff in this type of illegal activity is simply profit. Obtaining drugs on the streets is a costly habit as it is and the price is even higher when the transactions involves a deal made behind prison bars. Most officers who become involved in the drug economy work for a major dealer who is running a drug trafficking operation within the institution. Often, they will become involved through their knowledge of inmate associates on the streets. Through interviews and my own observations of inmate-staff relations, I came to be aware of the fact that Inmates are also keenly aware of how to recruit prospective officers. They are well aware of who is corrupt and who is not. They know who will "sell out" and who will turn them in. After all, corrupt officers will readily express feelings of animosity towards the administration. They do not attempt to hide from the inmates their disgust and lack of loyalty to the system. An inmate gave me an example of how to perceive a certain situation:

> you see a hack (officer) coming in here everyday with a bunch of gold rings and chains. He talks about how he bought his old lady some fancy clothes and jewelry. They're stupid enough you know, they love to boast. Then you hear from someone that officer has a real bitch car, like a Mercedes or something, maybe a sports car. The same person is always talking about how much he hates his job and how unfair the upper level white shirts are to him. And so on...you get the picture. ...now how is some fool who makes less than $20,000 a year getting all those goodies. Either he won the lottery or he does like all the others do...he's into drugs and he's hungry...for more goodies (Inmate, Central).

A typical transaction is set up whereby the officer meets with an associate of the inmate somewhere in the community. He is supplied with a certain amount of drugs and then the only thing left is for him to bring it to work. The officer usually does not make any type of payments to the street contact, as this is taken care of through other means by the inmate. The officer smuggles the drugs into the prison and then arranges to give it to the inmate at some pre-arranged time and location to minimize risk of detection. Depending on the amount, the officer will receive different types of rewards in terms of goods, services, or money.

The Lieutenant investigating staff corruption at Central told me that often, some naive officer will become involved in drug trafficking with inmates through extortion. An inmate will buddy up to the officer and ask him to do some small favor for him. In return he will do some favor for the officer such as providing him with extra help in his work duties or some contraband food item. After a relationship develops, the inmate will continue to ask for special favors and the officer will continue to comply. What is important in this cycle is that each request made by the inmate involves and requires increasingly more rule breaking activity. The officer is now is a position whereby he feels threatened by the inmate who makes him well aware of his position of violation with regard to the administrative rules and regulations. The inmate is now able to request any favor from the officer, even smuggling drugs into the institution, as he is threatened by the inmate unless he complies with his request. As a lieutenant put it, the officer "is in the pocket of the inmate."

Beyond drug trafficking, my research of prison organization further revealed another undercover world, a world of loan-sharking and prostitution, a highly covert and illegal world of activities which some officers become a part of. A Captain described to me a loan-sharking operation run by an officer who is currently under investigation:

> ...we got some officers here who run some big-time loan-sharking businesses. They're no doubt corrupt officers and a real disgrace because they take advantage of the inmates and encourage their illegal activities. What he does [the loanshark] is find out which inmates are desperate for money to payoff a debt, whether its gambling or drugs, or whatever. They can find that out easily, from other inmates or from the inmates' account. The officer approaches the inmate when he is alone and tells him he is aware of his problem and that he wants to help him. He'll make it sound real good, that he doesn't have to worry about getting into trouble because he's dealing with staff. The rate of return or interest rate is 100 percent but the inmate usually accepts the offer because he's desperate. The officer will

give him a month or two to pay off the debt. And he better pay it off, he knows that, and he usually does (Captain, Central).

The inmate in that type of situation, the Captain explained, is particularly vulnerable. He is threatened not only by the individual to which he owes the money but by the loan shark who just happens to be an officer with access to official administrative sanctions and unofficial sanctions that he may have imposed on other inmates.

The officer who runs a loan-sharking business usually does it for profit. He often has a steady flow of cash to run the operation, and he most likely has many contacts with inmates. He also probably involved in some type of illegal activity on the street. This type of officer is very much feared and abhorred but at the same time respected by the inmates, for he is able to strike a unique balance between law and order and law and disorder. He is not suspected by prison officials as being involved in any type of illegal activity because he appears to be very 'straight.' He performs all his duties with care and urgency, he acts strict and tough towards the inmates, and he usually runs a smooth clean shift because of the cooperation he receives from the inmates.

The dynamics of interaction between inmates and staff members revealed a wide array of love relationships developing between female officers and inmates. However, another type of relationship that was found to exist in the world of close interaction between the guard and the inmate, involves prostitution. Female officers involved in this activity take advantage of the vulnerability of the inmates and prostitute their bodies to make some extra money or get some favors from the inmates. Investigating officers looking into incidents of prostitution describe the female officers in such relationships as being particularly vulnerable, with low self-esteem and often poorly educated. Inmate informants also told me that these women are most likely desperate for money to support a drug or drinking habit and at the same time take care of several children. The relationship between the officer who is a prostitute and the inmate who is her client is symbiotic, "just the way it go on the streets," an inmate explained, "we both need something and we both use each other to get what we need." The inmate therefore does not look for a long-term relationship neither does he want one to develop. He is not looking to play upon the emotions of the officer to get her to fall in love with him and thus do him many favors, as do other inmates. He is simply looking for a means to release his sexual frustrations and sees the officer as an individual who is willing to provide him with this need for a payment in return. The inmate will give the officer money, jewelry, cigarettes, drugs, food and other items, depending on the services rendered by the officer. The officer must be careful though in soliciting inmates for the purpose of prostitution, for not all or even most of them are willing to engage in such activity. An inmate recounted to me the following incident underscoring this point:

> ...she [officer] came up to me one day while I was in the dorm folding my laundry. I had been here for around two months. I wasn't too surprised because some of the other guys were joking once with her and they later told me she was a freak. She said she could show me a good time and that it wouldn't cost me that much either. I told her that she better get her ass out of my dorm and that I wasn't that kind of guy who pay for having sex with nobody. I didn't threaten her but I could have if I wanted to. But she was real mad, I could tell...she was real mad. You see, these freaks look for guys with a lot of stuff; they want the guys with the fancy shoes and the big radios because they know they can get something good out of. But not all the guys here are willing to stoop that low, I mean don't get me wrong, there are alot of desperate guys who'll do anything to have sex...with anybody... but...not me (Inmate, Central).

Discretion is indeed important and officers involved in relationships with inmates revolving around covert, illegal activities, especially drug trafficking, must operate within an environment of closely monitored, controlled interactions (Marquart and Roebuck, 1985; Fleisher, 1989). The need arises for the emergence of a system of snitching which allows both officers and inmates to be aware of the potential threat and danger that may disrupt the control and order of their activities. This system of complex networking is similar in structure to the system of social control described by Marquart and Roebuck, and operates as a means of management whereby the role of the snitch becomes one of an informant or trustee more than the abhorred "rat" who squeals on other inmates (Marquart and

Roebuck, 1985). However, I discovered that the role of the informant goes beyond the gathering of information on ordinary inmate activities and rule violations (Marquart and Roebuck, 1985).

Informants are selected very carefully, as they must play a very dangerous role for the inmates and officers involved in the illegal business. They are usually inmates with official access to key places on the compound due to their work assignment, academic classes, recreational and religious activities. They must be familiar and trusted by alot of inmates for they are often in a position where they are eavesdropping on several conversations and at the same time trying to manipulate inmates to solicit information from them. They must also be friendly with and trusted by the administrative staff, for in many cases, they must obtain information on surprise shakedowns, on investigations of certain individuals, and on who is telling whom what and when they said it. The officer involved in the illegal activity usually relies on the inmate he is dealing with to select another inmate to act as an informant. The inmate knows who he can trust, for he has had alot of experience. It must be somebody whom he has known for a long time in prison, and preferably someone whom he knew from the street. They probably "hang with the same people," as an inmate puts it, and are part of the same clique of friends. The informant is expected to tell all. He can show no other favoritism or loyalty to anyone else. Inmates agree that it is an "unspoken rule of the snitch system" that he must be loyal to whomever hired him and he must keep his eyes and ears open for that person alone. If he hears something, a plot or plan that threatens the persons he is working for, he is expected to report it immediately to the right source, regardless of the consequences it may bring for others. While the informant does not know the intricate details of the illegal transactions, he knows enough to be a potential source of disruption and even threat. Therefore, he must prove his loyalty to both the inmate and the officer before he is given his task. The ultimate test of loyalty is to see if the prospective informant will sacrifice his own personal good for that of the inmate who is testing him. An inmate described to me an elaborate test of this sort:

> ...me and another inmate, we wanted to know if this other guy would be right for the job. You see, I could tell right now if you could be my informant, because if a white shirt come and ask you tell me what that inmate was telling you in the interview or else you will get into trouble because you wasn't supposed to be talking to me, even if I asked you not to you probably would...but don't take it personal you don't even know me or give a shit about me, and that's the same way all these guys here feel about each other. Everyone look out for himself when it comes right down to it. The informant is different though, because he has to look out for you. So anyway, we decided to give him a little test to see how far he would go for us. We set him up with a false wrap that I don't need to get into...and he knew that we had set him up. We got one of the officers who know what's going on to try to put the squeeze on him to get some information out of him. He told him all he needed was a name and he'd get out of it...he said, man why do you want to cover the ass of someone else when yours is on the line. But he wouldn't budge. He kept quiet and told them that it was his fault and that he'd take the blame for it. Man, good old ----- he never said a word. Later on, we got a lieutenant, another one of ours to bail him out of the hole. He passed that goddamn test, and we told him we'd make it worth his while too. And believe me, he still works for us and we take good care of him (Inmate, Central).

I was told that informants are indeed paid well for their services, by both the inmate and the officer they are involved with. Officers provide such rewards as privileged dormitory status, preferred work duties, the best of clothing and accessories and, what is seen as most important by inmates, a favorable report on behalf of the informant in front of the parole board. Inmate payoffs to the informant are many but generally they include institutional privileges and favors. They are protected and provided with many luxury items such as cigarettes, radios, and home made 'shoots' or wine. They are sometimes rewarded with extra cash in their inmate accounts or money may be provided for their families on the streets.

Inmates becoming involved in the snitch system do it for more than the material rewards though. An inmate describes his buddy who plays the part of the informant as "doing it for the thrill...dude gets a rush knowing he can get someone 'iced' anytime and knowing he can get 'iced' too...bull-shitting the 'white-shirts' all the time." There are thus a great deal of other rewards that come with the role of the informant, including the reputation, excitement, danger, status and influence. The part of the informant is usually played by the young yet experienced inmate.

He is the one that is willing to be a spy, to play both sides of the team and to enjoy the fast life and dangerous endeavors. He builds a reputation of being well respected yet feared, for it is never known to whom he will report what was said or done. He has a special status amongst the inmates for they know that he has good relations with the administration and is well liked and trusted by them, while at the same time he is "playing them" or "conning one of the white shirts" as an inmate put it, into giving him some information.

The role of the informant is not however, an envied position. For, many times, he may be put in a position where he feels threatened by both the officer and the inmate whom he works for. On many occasions, as evidenced by sting operations revealing covert illegal activities, the snitch system will fall short of providing enough accurate and detailed information to expose investigations into the activities of certain suspected inmates and officers. The inmate and officer involved in the illegal operations will then put the blame on the informant for failing to do his duties with care and accuracy, making him feel that it is his fault and thus they will threaten him with exposure. Essentially, they will let him take the fall for them if the authorities get too close and he will become the scapegoat for the whole group...the same people he once served so faithfully and the same people that once took good care of him and relied on his services to get out of many jams. Under this type of pressure, many informants will stay loyal to their employers. They feel that in the long run, they will be taken care of or 'bailed out' of the problem and they will resume their position once again. They also may do it out of fear, after all, they have everything to lose by betraying those individuals they once served faithfully. Not only will their role and activities in the illegal operations be exposed to the authorities, but it will, an inmate emphasizes, " be spread like fire throughout the compound" that such and such inmate became a snitch, a real snitch, someone who works for the administration. And in such a case, the inmate will be a target of anger, violence, and revenge, all which work together to create a recipe for sure destruction and even death, where, as an inmate put it,

> protective custody here at central don't mean a thing...it just means they'll take you out of
> sight for a while and maybe even transfer you till they forget about your case...but your
> enemies will never forget what you done. They'll make sure you pay, no matter how long
> you are locked down, or where they take you, they'll get to you and you'll always have to be
> looking over your shoulder because if you don't one day you'll find a knife in your back
> and that's if your lucky and they don't do something more horrifying than that (Inmate,
> Central).

In some cases, though, the informant will feel cornered by an investigating
officer. The officer, usually a lieutenant, will tell the inmate that he has so much
to lose by remaining silent. He will tell him that he will be doing more time than
he imagined and that he would probably go behind the wall [the dreadful
Maximum Security facility] where a lot of hard core criminals would "love to get
a shot at his ass." He will tell him he'll probably never make parole because he'll
see that he doesn't and that he could even see to it that he never walk the streets
again. The inmate already feels betrayed by the individuals he once loyally served,
who now are threatening him to take the fall for them and who have now turned
their backs on him. Furthermore, he is being threatened by the upper levels of the
administration. With the mounting pressure, then, occasionally, an informant will
break the snitch system code of silence and agree to provide the authorities with
his help in finding the key leaders of an illegal operation. The investigator will
manipulate the inmate to "get the most amount of juice possible out of him." He
will promise him special treatment and protection and usually, this promise is
kept. The chief of records told me that inmate informants will often be transported
to a federal institution that is far away and that has a tight security system, where
they can just"disappear out of site." On occasion, if the inmate is close to being
paroled, they will recommend that he be released and put into a witness protection
program. The inmate however, must still live with the overshadowing nightmare
of being a traitor, of selling out to the authorities, with the haunting words, "I'll get
you," and "you're a dead man," echoing in his ears for many years to come.

Relations developing between inmates and staff members are indeed reflective of the unique and situational characteristics of those daily activities and interactions that develop and shape the course of attitudes, behaviors and roles that each come to adopt. However, the picture would not be complete without an understanding of how these relations and interactions between inmates and staff come to influence patterns of interaction that develop amongst staff members with one another. I wish to turn now to a brief description of staff relations, in the hope that it would further shed some light on the dynamics of social organization prevalent in the modern correctional setting.

Guards Behind Bars: Staff-Staff Relations

A dominant theme that developed throughout my interviewing and surveying of correctional officers is the associated stresses and tensions that naturally accompany the job requirement of a correctional officer. The negative environment of the correctional officer stems from many sources. The most prevalent perceived by officers is their duties regarding the inmates in their custody. The problems associated with these duties revolves around an apprehension with the ever present physical danger of the prison environment along with the abusive treatment directed to them by the inmates, and the consequent mental stresses that result from these dynamics (Bowker, 1980; Lombardo, 1981; Crouch, 1991).

The correctional officer represents to the inmate the unfairness and injustices of the administration. They become the target of the inmates' hatred and frustrations as their enforcement of the rules is seen as biased, arbitrary and nonsensical. Correctional officers are the most frequent victims of inmate assaults, large scale acts of violence and retaliation (Bowker, 1980; Fleisher, 1989). Moreover, it is very difficult for them to do their job, for their precise role is often unclear, undefined and not discernable. They are expected to be many different things all at once, with these expectations often clashing or contradicting one another. The officer is supposed to be a gatekeeper, an upholder of the law and a supporter of discipline and order. Yet, he is also expected to cater to the needs of a demanding and overbearing population who do not always comply with the rules and regulations. He is a counselor who is expected to use a treatment and rehabilitative approach and must listen to the complaints, hurts, needs and grumbles of those under his care. Yet, he is also an authority figure, a custodian or a policeman who must remain neutral in conflict situations to carry out the goals of prison security and control of the resident population.

In this tense and uncertain environment, the correctional officer experiences role conflict and therefore finds great difficulty in doing his many tasks throughout the daily routine, and interaction with co- workers is inevitably made more difficult and laborious. This is further complicated by the shortage of staff whereby inmates significantly outnumber staff and the rate of incarceration is constantly going up (Bowker, 1980). Increasing litigation by inmates against staff members for alleged abuse, neglect and violation of rules and procedures has also placed an added stress on correctional officers, for this diminishes their capability to exercise control in a situation that might call for a unique diversion from the rules. Correctional officers are thus placed in a position where they are forced to take on very tight work shifts, with multiple tasks being repetitious, lengthy, and demanding (Crouch and Marquart, 1980; Lombardo, 1981; Jurik, 1985; DiIulio, 1987). They feel powerless, under payed, dissatisfied and unable to exercise the discretion needed to efficiently run a correctional facility. There is a lack of support from administrators, supervisors and even other officers in the constant struggle to overcome feelings of chaos, powerlessness and the approval of the disciplinary handling of inmates (Lombardo, 1981; Crouch, 1991). A staff member explains:

> ...I guess I was the new rookie officer and they put me on a shift that was impossible. I was doing my own duties in my dormitory, plus, I was standing the mess, monitoring the commissary line and participating in shakedowns. All of this was in one day and one right after the other...it was just too much because each of these situations represent so much conflict between the inmates with each other and towards the officer. You can have...well...like a fight at the commissary, another encounter at the mess and possibly you can run into some trouble during the shakedown because that always makes them real nervous and defensive. Too much contact between officers and inmates is no good. Sometimes, you are just waiting for an inmate to push you too far so you can really get

him. You learn to ignore it most of the time buy you're only human and you can only take so much crap. There should be enough staff to keep it rotating so that it is kept to a minimum. But there isn't and there isn't a single officer or supervisor that would care about what you're going through everyday. You have to step back once in a while and get away somewhere behind a desk...pretend you're a big shot white shirt who doesn't have to do those "dirty jobs" like standing the mess hall. Then you can get yourself together (Corporal, Central).

With these frustrations mounting, there prevails a strong competition amongst staff members to move up to higher positions within the prison ranks. For, everyone is trying to get out of the bottom ranks to escape the long hours, stressful work assignments, dangers, abuses and hardships associated with the job of an officer (Lombardo, 1981; Crouch, 1991). Promotion to a higher rank means more privileges for the staff member and more privileges means less problems or crises to be encountered on a daily basis.

However, the competition for advancement tends to harbor and encourage the development of an attitude of suspicion, jealousy and mistrust, which make it seem like staff members are working against each other, instead of working with one another to reach a common goal. During my research, I attended several staff cook-outs, fund-raisers, competitive sporting events, and picnics. During these events, I observed the way in which different staff members interact with one another. They seemed somewhat congenial and polite to one another. Some kept a professional distance from one another, while others joked around and carried on like old friends. Something, however, struck my attention when I overheard two male staff members talking about one of the female staff members, making strong sexual comments about her and looking her up and down. I could not tell what positions these individuals occupied, for although I became familiar with the various rankings, at this time, all staff members were out of uniform. However, I recognized one of the men as a correctional officer and the female as a unit manager. The female staff member seemed to be aware of what they were doing but did not appear to be bothered. One of the men made a direct comment to her which I could not hear. He apparently said something with a slight bit of humor and sarcasm that made her begin to joke around with him in an attempt to retaliate in a joking manner. All of a sudden, I saw the male staff member approach the female and grab her chest. She began to laugh and commented, "don't make me jump you now." Four other officers were standing around and laughing.

This encounter seemed to be very strange to me. I felt like the relationships between staff members went beyond a nine to five job that ended when the day was over. There had to be some kind of unique characteristic that would allow such an exchange to take place. I decided to delve deeper into the world of the correctional officer in order to understand the dynamics of interaction that drives the various relationships that exist. A lieutenant introduced me to this world with the following comments:

> You come here everyday and have to face so much as a correctional officer. There are so many things wrong with the administration. And you have to deal with rude people all the time, inmates and staff. It seems that instead of officers influencing inmates to behave good, the attitude of the inmates rubs off on the staff...probably because they get too involved with them. There is so much gossip, jealousy, and corruption amongst staff. Everybody looks to everyone else and wants to be better. You can't really trust no one and that is why I choose not to socialize with anyone. I just come here and do my job and go home and forget about it...you can't carry this type of job home with you; otherwise, the whole thing would get to me and I would start treating my friends in the same rude way I see people here treating each other...and that's no way to live (Lieutenant, Central).

Relationships between staff members exist at various levels. On March 5, 1995, the *Washington Post* reported that a class action suit was filed against the D.C. Department of Corrections for sexual harassment. On April 21, 1995, a jury awarded plaintiffs 1.425 million dollars in damages (Neal et al. v Dir. DCDC et al., #93-2420 DDC). A very prevalent issue, thus, that is dominant among and addressed by all the ranks is that of sexual harassment, an issue that is rarely discussed, if not completely ignored in the literature on prison social organization. From the moment a female becomes hired by the administration as a correctional officer, counselor, case manager, or other employee, she becomes the target of a series of games played by male staff members, starting from the top ranks all the way down to the bottom. The EEO (Equal Employment Opportunity) officer explains:

117

A new woman around here means a chance for someone to get her into bed. From the moment she steps into the facility she is treated like a queen...they buy her lunch everyday, bring her flowers, give her time off and so on, things like that. Then they'll invite her to some event, a party, where they'll tell her they're throwing her a party so she can get to know everyone. The party will be in an apartment and only men will be there...probably mostly white shirts and higher up people in the administration. They know her weakness, like maybe she drinks a little too much. Then they'll get her drunk. One of the white shirts there will make a move on her...we have this lady here who was at that sort of party and two of the men there asked her if she wanted to have sex with them, you know, what they call a turkey sandwich. She was too drunk to know what was going on so she agreed to go upstairs with them. After they got started, she told them to stop, that she was hurting. Then she began to cry because she was in pain and bleeding...I still have that case because the next day, she came to me and told me what had happened and I convinced her to file a complaint against them because that was considered rape. That rarely happens though...usually they get away with it. ...women who come new here, well, it's like...it's like a deck of cards, where the white shirts are the aces and after they get through with a woman they pass her down the ranks to the kings, jacks, all the way to the 2's, and everyone gets a shot at her. It's really pathetic... really sick (Officer, Central).

This type of sexual harassment is commonplace and the complaints are many. There are various factors that may precipitate, facilitate and encourage the occurrence of such deviant interaction between male and female staff members. A major contributor to the incidence of sexual harassment within the prison institution is the stresses that already exist within the incarcerated society. Female correctional officers described to me a world where the fierce competition between staff members and the lack of solidarity produces a strong sense of isolation and alienation. The opportunities for advancement are very limited and support from supervisors is almost lacking. Female officers, especially, are treated coldly and with suspicion by other female staff members who see them as a potential threat to their own positions. The sudden attention from top level officers is therefore seen as a welcome opportunity to make connections with the right people and is also perceived as a means to make friends in a somewhat unfriendly environment. Some women are thus, an officer explains, "willing to sacrifice their own dignity and self-respect in order to get ahead." The prison environment also fosters an extreme power differential between lower rank correctional officers and lieutenants and captains, or "white-shirts" as they are called. Many officers expressed the view that the correctional officer is looked

118

upon by higher officials in the administration as being incompetent and incapable of making decisions on his own. They are allowed very little input in making or influencing changes in work conditions and institutional assignments, procedures to more effectively monitor and control the inmate population, and other important administrative decisions (EEO, Central). This harbors feelings of resentment and inferiority. The consequent lack of self-esteem and low job status assigned to the role of the correctional officer is also heightened by any personal problems the female officer may have. These factors work together to create an atmosphere that is conducive to the breeding of sexual harassment.

Finally, the prison environment itself contributes to a large extent to the paths of interaction that staff members take with each other. The dormitory style prison system calls for staff members, especially officers, being in very close proximity to the inmates. I observed that unit managers, psychologists, case workers, correctional officers and counselors are all located throughout the compound either inside dormitories or right next to them, with inmates coming in and out all day. Thus, this closed, almost homogeneous surrounding makes it difficult if not impossible to separate the world of the inmates from the world of the staff. Each day, officers and other staff witness many atrocities. Profanity, assault, harassment, insults, violence and other negative behaviors become, as I myself witnessed, commonplace. A psychologist expounds upon the effect of such an environment on staff work relations:

> working in corrections is a different experience than working any place else. In a regular office type job setting, you come in everyday and everybody says good morning to everybody. Even your enemies manage to squeeze out a smile. People are civilized and they abide by the rules of common courtesy...of normal society. But it's different here; the rules of society as you and I know it don't exist. This is a society of people with no humane rules. You never make good friends because one day they'll be the same people that stick a knife in your back. No one gets respect so no one gives respect. Prison has an ambiance of violence, intimidation and hostility. The catch is though, is that these values flourish because many of the staff here come to adopt the same attitudes as the residents and these behavior patterns are carried into the normal work day and in the normal course of interaction between staff (Psychologist, Central).

We have thus far seen that Central is a modern prison where a diverse and not so diverse population of inmates, correctional officers, psychologists, counselors, case workers, unit managers, and administrators interact with one another on a daily basis to constitute the miniature society we all know as the prison institution. This society operates according to its own formal rules, procedures and regulations which are deliberately designed and implemented to accomplish certain goals. However, informal practices emerge which become incorporated into and sometimes even change the formal structure of the organization. The organization of a prison, as any other institution does not operate strictly by the formal rules or procedures of the bureaucratic blueprint. Informal systems emerge that shape and sometimes even compromise the formal system. Interaction amongst members of this society is thus dictated by the informal structure of the prison, and is driven by the learning and internalizing of the cultural and societal aspects, the various roles, attitudes, activities and behaviors, which, along with the structural forces driving these phenomena, constitute the social organization of the modern prison.

I wish to turn now to a detailed analysis of the many observations and descriptions I have been making thus far. I wish to examine in greater depth, several questions which will attempt to highlight some of this prison's unique characteristics.

CHAPTER 6: LORTON CENTRAL: ANALYSIS OF THE DATA

Prison is a place where inmates are confined in an all encompassing social environment whose characteristics contradict the goals of reform and rehabilitation. Upon entry into prison, inmates are deprived of their personal possessions, stripped, searched, disinfected, issued an identification number, assigned to a dormitory or cell block and re-socialized for life behind bars, being placed at the mercy of and under the absolute control of a hierarchy of officials. This begins the process of dehumanization and forced helplessness described at lengths by Clemmer, Sykes, Goffman, Irwin and others, whereby the inmate is seen as child-like, inferior and deplorable and is treated accordingly.

Throughout my research, I observed a great deal of this process of dehumanization. An incident was recalled to me by the IGP (Inmate Grievance Procedure) Officer. There was a complaint filed by an inmate against an officer. The following incident was reported by the inmate:

> During the afternoon count one day, the officer on duty came to me and told me to pull down my pants. I asked him why and he said it was none of my business that he was going to do a rectal search for drugs. I told him he was making a big mistake and that I wasn't hiding no drugs and told him he had no right doing that, especially with no reason and in front of all those other inmates. He paid no attention and I pulled my pants down and bent over for him and right in front of a hundred other inmates he did the exam. It was so humiliating and the only thing that made me keep my nerve was that I kept telling myself he wouldn't get away with it... (Inmate, Central).

The prison institution operates according to its own system of stratification, its own cultural norms and rules, and its own unique language and social roles (Trestar, 1981). There are both formal and informal guidelines for appropriate behavior. There are also ways to accommodate to the extreme power differential between the oppressor and the oppressed, where power is not always in the hands of formal authority. Upon entry into prison, an inmate must become familiar with the new rules and expected roles in his new setting as the old ones are no longer relevant. This means that prisoners must become aware of the formal system of specific rules and procedures provided and enforced by prison authorities. There is also an informal system that inmates must learn, those unwritten guidelines and norms for acceptable and unacceptable behaviors in interacting with guards and other inmates.

Prisons are organized as bureaucratic agencies, with inmates being the inevitable customers. Authority is arranged hierarchically, with a well defined chain of command (Trestar, 1981). There is the warden, assistant warden, captain, lieutenant, sergeant, corporal and trainee. The main goal of this bureaucracy is control of the inmate population, where order is imposed by the authorities through the use of force or threat of harsh sanctions. Control of the inmates depends on the complete structuring of their lives, which is perceived by inmates as for the good of the institution rather than for their own good, safety, protection or welfare. Deprivation is also a form of violence administered by prison authorities as inmates are placed in prolonged solitary confinement, and sometimes, food withheld from them (Marquart, 1986). The organization of a prison, as any other institution, does not operate strictly by the formal rules or procedures of the formal administration. Rather, the data reveals that the social organization of the modern prison is marked by an informal system of control, a world of roles and interactions that come to shape and sometimes even compromise the formal system. Administrative rules and convict rules sometimes clash, and inmates must choose which way to follow. If the administration catches an inmate abiding by the informal convict system, then they will make him pay by sending him to the hole or detention unit. And, if an inmate is caught abiding by the formal rules of the administration, then his fellow convicts will retaliate with verbal abuse, destroying or taking his personal property and violent acts of physical torture. Within the informal system, prisoners come to control much of life in the custodial institution. The patterns of behavior that come to occupy much of the social organization of the prison can be called the inmate social system, a system which has come to be marked by increasing violence, fear and anger, a system where, as one inmate put it,

> ...people don't just let things go...that's not prison culture; all disputes must be settled. I saw a man get killed at Lorton over who discovered America (Inmate, Central).

Previous studies of the prison community have developed around a concern for the sociological analysis of the prison as a social system. The works of Clemmer, Schrag, Cressey, Sykes, Irwin and others have all focused on the social structure, roles, and value systems of the inmate population. The findings of these studies point to an inmate social system that is perpetuated by a set of norms and values that are anti-social and that contradict the goals of the prison administration. Inmate behavior is dictated by a normative structure that values criminal behavior and that is consistent with a criminal sub-culture. Although categories of roles and behavior patterns emerge within the inmate social system, the prison community is by and large divided, with prisoners acting in isolation or in small groups.

However, it is not enough to say that the inmate social system is characterized by a normative structure which values criminal behavior. A comprehensive analysis of the prison community must evaluate the dynamics of the prison system with an emphasis on those structural elements of prison social organization that shape the course of interaction between inmates and staff. Throughout this analysis, we will attempt to accomplish this task.

As stated previously, inmates entering prison are degraded, deprived and dehumanized. Reactions to this process varies from prisoner to prisoner. Some withdraw and react with passivity and seclusion. Others may go to the opposite extreme, rebelling against the system and fighting back at very opportunity. Then there are those inmates who accommodate or adjust to the system, trying to make the best out of a bad situation. Regardless of the individual patterns of response to incarceration, inmates must go through a process of learning and internalizing the culture of the inmate social system (Fleisher, 1989).

Like any other social system, the inmate social system contains norms for appropriate behavior which are enforced by various social control devices. A major goal of this informal system is to alleviate the various social, psychological and material deprivations of the inmates. Characteristic of the contemporary inmate social system is the stratification within its population based on gang membership and economic activity. Inmates who belong to gangs with more control over the contraband economy have a higher status in the prison social organization. This higher status creates a system of stratification whereby the powerful dominate the weak and are able to manipulate and control interaction within the inmate social system. It also creates the possibility of large-scale episodes of violence as gang warfare erupts in the struggle for power, where power is based on the ability to successfully deliver contraband goods and services to the resident population.

With the expansion of the inmate contraband system, violent gangs have emerged and have come to dominate all aspects of inmate economic and social activity (Irwin, 1980; Colvin, 1992). The proliferation of drugs in prison has bred the need for the emergence of a system of control to manage the expansive and risky transactions of the inmate drug economy. Drug trafficking in prison has heightened the incidence of violence, fear and suspicion within the inmate social system, coupled with a marked reduction in inmate solidarity (Fleisher, 1989). Gangs become involved in disputes over drug deals and in robbing drug dealers. Large scale retaliation in the form of threats, beatings, torture, hostility, and blood shed are rampant. Power struggles inevitably occur, and the prison administration must interfere in order to maintain a certain degree of control over the inmate population. Sykes observed in The Society of Captives (1958) that the prison system is undermined by the corruption of authority. He noted that, a guard cannot rely on the direct application of force to achieve compliance nor can he easily depend on threats of punishment. The guard is under pressure to achieve a smoothly running tour of duty not with the stick but with the carrot, but here again his legitimate stock is limited; he finds that one of the most meaningful rewards he can offer is to ignore certain offenses. Thus the guard...often discovers that his best path of action is to make 'deals' or 'trades' with the captives in his power. In effect, the guard buys compliance or obedience in certain areas at the cost of tolerating disobedience elsewhere (Sykes, 1958). The realities of Sykes' observations are particularly relevant to the structure of the modern prison. The prison administration realizes the relative impossibility of enforcing all the rules, all the time due to the shortage in staff and the dynamics of prison overcrowding. Officials are well aware of the rampant flow of drugs and other contraband in prison and they know that inmates are not going to obey the rules because of a strong loyalty to their own gang organizations. Accordingly, prison officials cannot achieve their primary objective of controlling the inmate population by relying on force alone to compel inmates to abide by the rules. The dynamics of prison organization call for the overlooking of some rule breaking activities, thereby achieving complacency on the part of the resident population, in return for overall order. The administration regards some rule violation as beneficial for the successful operation of the institution. The contraband system provides inmates with an environment that makes prison life more tolerable and therefore they are less likely to be hostile towards prison personnel. Thus, in resolving the apparent structural contradiction between the law enforcement goals of the administration and the need for inmates to operate contraband systems, a compromise is reached whereby, in practice, the prison achieves order by tolerating disorder (Chambliss, 1988).

Going a step beyond, the intricate dynamics of prison organization have evolved around the participation of prison officials in inmate illegal activities, which actually becomes a constant source of control within the inmate social system (Lombardo, 1980; Fleisher, 1989). Illegal transactions, and especially drug trafficking, are organized along a hierarchy of gang activity, with prison officials involved at all levels. Inmates manipulate the involvement of officers in their illegal activities to their advantage. They use the officers as an inside source to get information on snitches, surprise shakedowns and sting operations, while at the same time threatening to expose them if they discontinue their cooperation. Moreover, the involvement of officials in inmate illegal activities produces a further damaging effect on prison management that is exploited by inmates, as it creates a conflict between staff members who are suspicious, resentful and uncooperative with one another. On the other hand, officers involved in drug trafficking use their knowledge of the inmates' illegal activities to create a de facto prison management that is based on the relationship between inmates and guards (Fleisher, 1989). The guards' access to the sub rosa economy is used by them as a threat to retaliate against the inmates for lack of cooperation, and thereby regaining power and controlling any large-scale attempts at violence against the administration (Irwin, 1980).

Moreover, the loss of formal control over the prison has led guards to use gang leaders as a source of informal control over the inmates (Irwin, 1980). Inmate leaders of illegal rackets such as drug trafficking have a vested interest in maintaining an orderly institution as a disruption in the status quo would pose a risk to their operations. Thus, the tolerance for drug trafficking and other illegal activities was the result of a series of informal compromises which meant overlooking certain infractions as trade-offs for the appearance of order in the operation of the dormitories, and the prison in general (Fleisher, 1989; Colvin, 1992). Eventually, however, a disruption occurs in the pattern of interaction: an FBI investigation exposes the corruption, a snitch makes a deal with the authorities, gang warfare breaks out and the prison administration begins to crack down on formerly acceptable or overlooked behaviors and conditions among the inmates. But in doing this, there results a disruption in the social relationships, structure and roles within the inmate social structure (Crouch, 1980; Colvin, 1992). Changes in resident leadership patterns add to the lack of stability and create a climate of chaos. Other means by which prison authorities retrieve control from inmates are to increase the use of solitary confinement, breakup gangs by transferring inmates to other facilities, and increase security searches (Irwin, 1980; Crouch, 1980).

As former sources of inmate power are removed, a struggle for power between rival gang members emerges, which becomes increasingly based on violence, as alternative sources of non-violent power are diminished (Fleisher, 1989; Irwin, 1980). Thus, the competition to establish a violent reputation, the most important source of power in prison, in turn generates more violence and warfare (Irwin, 1980). The willingness and ability to engage in violent, predatory behavior arises from the structural reality of prison organization. The operation of the prison system calls for the encouragement of predatory behaviors by prison administrators as a means of social control (Lockwood, 1980; Marquart and Roebuck, 1985). After all, the more that the prison population is divided, the less likely inmates will unite to threaten the official control of the prison. Thus, a violent reputation becomes the best and only means of protection against other inmates. The only other alternatives are submission or seeking the protection of the prison administration. However, inmates generally agree that these two alternatives contain worse consequences than fighting and forming self-protection groups with other inmates. The result is a social environment with a never ending climate of violence, fear and tension (Lockwood, 1980).

Violence is primarily channeled through the behaviors and activities of prison gangs. The degree of inmate solidarity may vary from prison to prison, and even within a single prison. In the history of a single prison, there may be times of strong cohesion among the inmates while at other times the inmate social structure may be fragmented into small, warring groups. The penetration of gangs

127

into the prison social structure has had a strong impact on the dynamics of prison organization. Whereas in the past, inmate activities were dominated by a few powerful prison leaders, inmates are now factionalized into gangs, each with their own set of values, ideals and expectations (Irwin, 1980; Fleisher, 1989; Colvin, 1992). This has created tension within the inmate population as gang membership divides inmates, encouraging the clashing of interests, diversity, hatred and even prejudice within this unique, racially homogeneous population of inmates. These findings are significant in light of the fact that most studies of prison organization point to the racial source of inmate fragmentation (Carroll, 1974; Jacobs, 1977; Irwin, 1980; Fleisher, 1989), whereas my examination of Central shows that fragmentation can be pervasive even in a racially homogeneous institution, and based on gangs rather than racial groups. Thus, the very source of group identity, support and definition, actually serves to create divisions within the inmate community and cause the prison population to be disorganized. The effect is a breakdown in the morale among inmates, which is detected by the administration and is seen as a threat to the stability of the structure of the prison (Fleisher, 1989; Colvin, 1993). Prison officials react by "beefing up" security, monitoring gang activity, reducing inmate movement within the prison and in general taking measures to avoid a disruption in the social relations of the prison community. Nonetheless, the forming of gangs provides inmates with the opportunity to band together in groups to share common grievances and to develop ideas on how to collectively beat the system. Animosity towards the administration is thus heightened as individual thoughts are able to be expressed collectively.

Gangs provide inmates with opportunities for obtaining illegal goods and services, with protection and support in settling "beefs," with a sense of commitment, identity and a reputation. Membership in a gang is largely based on the ability to create and maintain a violent reputation. Inmates will do anything to gain the respect of their peers, including taking the risk of a prolonged sentence for stabbing someone, just to make themselves a reputation. Gangs are made up of inmates who used to "run together on the streets," which makes them tighter and more likely to stick together. The prevalence of gangs in prison escalates violence in the settling of "beefs." Whereas in the past a dispute between two inmates was settled in a very specific and individualistic manner, with gangs, the whole group gets involved in the problem, increasing the chances of getting the whole incident blown out of proportion (Irwin, 1980). The following incident described by an inmate illustrates this point:

> a young member of the Moors Muslim religious gang came to the dormitory on afternoon and found another inmate lying down on the top bunk above him. He told him to get up because he was going to do his afternoon prayer and that he had to be alone. The inmate explained that he was not feeling well and that he had to come back to the dormitory early from his work detail and that he was not going to get up for anybody and that he had a right to be there in his own bed. The Muslim Moor inmate asked him again to leave or else he would retaliate against him badly. The inmate ignored him and continued to sleep in his bed. Later on that evening, the Muslim Moor inmate went to the leader of the gang and described to him the incident. The leader told him that this was a great act of disrespect on the part of the other inmate not to get up for him so he could do the afternoon prayer. The leader told him not to worry about it that he would take care of the problem. A few days later, while the inmate who would not get up was in the bathroom washing his face, four members of the Muslim Moor group approached him and told him we will teach you to respect the Muslim faith. They beat him up so badly, I heard you couldn't even recognize who he was. His arm was broken and several ribs. Of course several other inmates saw what happened but no one would dare get involved to tell the authorities what happened...you just don't do that here (Inmate, Central).

Gang violence is further precipitated by the prevalence of younger inmates as members. Prison has become a breeding ground for inmates who are increasingly youthful and incorrigible to authority. An inmate described this situation:

> older inmates know how to stay cool under pressure; they know when to break down before the administration and when to stand up to them. They know the politics of prison...if you scratch my back, i'll scratch yours. Older inmates will section their time, plan it, schedule things, break it down...they do their time. Younger people let the time do them (Inmate, Central).

Consistent with Irwin's findings in support of importation theory, young inmates carry into prison the negative attitudes from the streets (Irwin, 1980). They form gangs based on old friendships and hang out together and encourage negative attitudes. Younger inmates lack initiative and personal thought and everything they do is based on what is socially accepted at Lorton and to their fellow gang members. The fear of losing their gang member status prevents them from getting involved in self- improving activities. I was told that it is "punk" to go to school, participate in religious activities and substance abuse programs, follow administrative rules or be nice to other people who are not part of your own gang. Young people lack the wisdom of older convicts and therefore they have great difficulty and often refuse to play the game of symbiotic relationship between inmates and officers. A disruption in the social structure of the prison organization occurs and threatens the stability of inmate and staff relations. Older gang members, usually leaders, must interfere to restore order and balance by eliminating troublesome youth. The result is the triggering of a series of vicious incidents of beatings, knifings and homicide where conflict oriented youth pitted against opposing gang leaders can turn the situation into a violent bloodbath.

Younger inmates do not act rationally or logically in settling "beefs," because they are caught up in trying to build a reputation for themselves that is based upon drug trafficking, violence, womanizing and dealing in the contraband economy. Conflict oriented young people are ready to kill just because someone stepped on his shoes or accidentally spilled some coffee on him. Kill or be killed is thus the attitude that comes to predominate prison life, an attitude which forms the basis for the convict code and convict identity (Braswell et al., 1985). The essence of social organization and interaction within the informal structure of the inmate social system is therefore dictated by the convict code which is shaped and formulated by the convict identity.

Irwin noted in <u>Prisons In Turmoil</u> (1980) that the social organization of the modern prison is in a state of division, tension and hostility (Irwin, 1980). He states that prisons are increasingly dominated by violent cliques and gangs who regularly rob and attack other inmates for the purposes of retaliation, stealing goods, building a reputation and seeking sexual favors. The new prison "hero" is that inmate who "is tough, and who is able to take care of himself in the prison world where people will attack others with little or no provocation...and [has] the guts to take from the weak" (Irwin, 1980: 193). Irwin attributes the escalation of murderous gangs, violence and attack in the modern prison to a disillusionment on the part of prisoners with the system of corrections. He argues that the ideals of rehabilitation are replaced by a convict identity that fosters a deep antagonism towards the prison administration, with its harsh, punitive approach, which comes to be viewed by inmates as the oppressor, the captor and the enemy (Irwin, 1980). An analysis of the data in the present study will go a step further to reveal the structural dynamics of the modern prison that have directed the course of interaction within the prison social system to create a new convict identity among prisoners. Violence and predatory behavior is an ever-present condition among inmate populations (Bowker, 19880; Braswell et al., 1985). This is true because of the very nature of the prison organization itself. Violence in prison can take on two forms, including violence between inmates and violence between inmates and guards. Violence between inmates takes several forms, including physical threats, verbal abuse, homosexual rape, beatings, torture and homicide (Bowker, 1980; Braswell et al., 1985).

An examination of the prison population will reveal that it is composed disproportionately of persons who have histories of aggressive and violently predatory behaviors, including murder, assault, rape, robbery and burglary (Saltzburg, 1993). At Central Prison, over 99% of the inmates are incarcerated for felony convictions, with an average of 12 previous arrests. These dynamics are further complicated and enhanced by the prison experience itself. Rage and frustration among inmates result from the conditions of imprisonment, including overcrowding, lack of privacy, the subjection to a constant threat of violence and danger and the abuse by prison guards and other staff members (Marquart and Roebuck, 1985). The structure of imprisonment calls for the confinement of large groups of inmates in an all-inclusive environment with a limited capacity. The

131

current ideology of justice and fairness which is caught up with wanting to incarcerate more individuals and for longer sentences has resulted in rapidly growing prison populations.

Overcrowding within the prison system is an additional burden whose brunt is borne by the individual inmate (DiIulio, 1987). The population of all individuals incarcerated under the jurisdiction of the D.C. Department of Corrections rose from 4,746 inmates in 1980 to 12,355 inmates in 1990 (D.C. Department of Corrections, Department of Analysis Office). Inmates under the conditions of overcrowding feel closed in, trapped and under constant surveillance, as they are forced to sleep side by side, share the same living space and breathe the same air. This close proximity has the added danger of deception. An inmate with drugs on him can stash them closer to the inmate's bed next to his, and if a shakedown occurs and the drugs are discovered, both inmates will suffer reprisal. Overcrowding also enhances the feelings of insecurity experienced by inmates, as the capability of guards to monitor the activities of such a large inmate population is drastically diminished. Inmates thus become more defensive, suspicious of other inmates and ready to attack at any sign of aggression. Security problems are heightened by the incidence of attack by inmates on other inmates to take their property, as there are not enough institutional goods to go around in plenty for everyone. Torn up clothes and bad shoes are not replaced and inmates must live with an insufficient supply of toilet paper, soap and other items necessary for personal hygiene. The deprivation of such basic human needs creates a strong sense of animosity towards the system as it represents a deliberate and moral rejection of the criminal by society. Frustration also occurs over the lack of enough programming for the entire inmate population, intensified by the lack of initiative on the part of teachers and instructors, and the long waiting lists to participate in educational and vocational training programs (Trestar, 1980; Fleisher 1989; Colvin, 1992).

Thus, the structure of prison life, along with its monotonous and boring tasks and routines, sexual frustrations, lack of motivating work, and the feeling of most prisoners that they have been victimized by the system, promotes a strong sense of resentment, bitterness and hostility towards one another and towards the administration where the recipe for explosive acts of violence is inevitable. Aggression, violence and animosity towards the administration therefore, form the basis of the convict identity. Thus, the convict ideal, far from carrying the attributes of cooperation, tolerance and leadership, is characterized by an unprecedented growth of convicts who despise, resent, distrust and attack other prisoners and the prison administration itself.

The patterns of interaction that emerge from the convict identity are expressed in the unspoken language of the inmate code of ethics known as the convict code. A convict code must develop to run the prison. Sykes states in The Society of Captives (1958) that,

> the development of special languages for special groups organized within the framework of the larger society is a phenomenon common in the social history of languages; pungent, vivid, racy and irreverent, the parlance of prisoners reflects the personality of the inmates who employ it, as well as the conflicts and tensions inherent in the institutional setting...it is the language of the dispossessed, tinged with bitterness and marked by a self-lacerating humor (Sykes, 1958: 84).

The importance of the convict code with regard to the organization of the prison lies in the fact that it provides a framework or map to maintain and reenforce the inmate social system. The rise in unruly, unregulated groups of younger prisoners, as Irwin notes, has obliterated the old convict code whose ethics centered on the ideas of leadership and power based on gaining the respect of other inmates (Irwin, 1980). The new gang-based convict code, which replaces the older inmate code, calls for the disrespect on the part of inmates of each other and of authority. The prison ethos is confrontation oriented where any spot within the prison is considered a potential zone for possible lethal retaliation. Younger inmates no longer settle "beefs" by talking it out with each other. Instead, the slightest move can be interpreted as a sign of disrespect and is met with a violent and sometimes deadly response.

Younger inmates are content with life in prison, as they see going to jail as merely a part of hustling on the streets. Moreover, their lives and activities in prison are increasingly coming to resemble their lives on the streets. Their girlfriends come to see them every week and occasionally they can sneak some sex. They have their old street buddies with them in the dormitory and they hang with the same gang. They can get their drugs whenever they want and get drunk when they want. They carry the same walk-mans and walk around with the same designer tennis shoes. They can sleep all day, loafing around doing nothing, and stay up at night playing cards or shooting pool.

These characteristics of prison life are met with the ideology in corrections that calls for sentences today that are longer than ever, an ideology which has undermined efforts at rehabilitation and subverted control (Saltzburg, 1993). Thus, with little incentive to participate in programs geared towards rehabilitation, inmates develop an "anything goes" attitude as they see no difference in how they behave while serving their time. Behavior becomes dictated by a code of ethics which values idleness, lawlessness and toughness where you can get killed for reading someone's mail, for borrowing someone's toothpaste, for cutting in front of someone in the phone line, for tripping someone in the mess hall or for nothing at all.

The convict code is designed to dictate behavior that is socially accepted within the inmate social system and is accepted by inmates and encouraged by guards as a means of internal control. Inmates must know the limits of doing wrong and balance the wrong with what's right in the eyes of the administration. Debts must be settled, stealing must be limited, respect must be given where and when it is due, and one must never drop his guard.

There are various "unspoken" laws which govern the convict code and the most basic rule is that which condemns snitching. Violence directed at suspected snitches is the most common source of bloodshed in prison, especially with the risks involved in the expansive drug rackets (Braswell et al., 1985). Snitching is unacceptable at any level and those who break the code of silence are regarded by inmates as the ultimate traitors and worthy of any punishment that will fall upon them. Closely related to snitching is the rule governing the over-fraternizing with staff. Inmates who give too much respect to authority and become too comfortable in the prison environment are seen as potentially dangerous.

The convict code places a strong emphasis on violent, predatory behavior. Thus, inmates become pre-occupied with building a reputation for toughness, callousness and brutality. This reputation is encouraged by the presence of territorial cliques who carry with them into the prison old neighborhood gang beefs. These gangs hate and distrust one another, harboring old hostilities that are often settled inside the prison. Their violence is not carried out in any organized fashion as the ever-present fear, suspicion and anxiety prevents inmates from acquiring solidarity and cohesion necessary for organized resistance. Instead, opposing cliques wage bloody war on each other and lash out at authority, assaulting one another and attacking staff members (Braswell et al., 1985; Fleisher, 1989). A violent reputation is a necessary and important part of the convict identity for several reasons. Consistent with the findings of Lockwood, violence is a means by which convicts establish their sexual identity (Lockwood, 1980). Inmates will verbally assault, stab, beat and even kill an inmate who makes a sexual pass at them. By attacking potential homosexuals who approach them, inmates make the public statement that they are opposed to homosexuality. They prevent future attacks by homosexual aggressors, and avoid the stigma of being labeled a "fag," thereby reaffirming their masculine identities. Thus, violence becomes a means of protection against future victimization and sexual assault.

Violence is also a means by which inmates show their belief in and loyalty to the new convict code (Lockwood, 1980). Interaction between inmates is based on hostility, predatory behavior, aggression and retaliation. Identification with the convict code calls for the response to threats with threats. Grievances must not be taken to staff members, for this is seen as a form of snitching. Matters of dispute are not settled through talking as this is seen to be a sign of weakness. Verbal communication and the willingness to negotiate a dispute is regarded as an attribute of someone who has not adopted the prison culture. This inmate can get into deep trouble as he is seen to be vulnerable and powerless. Thus, an inmate cannot look at a confrontation with the view that it may affect his appearance before the parole board. Instead, he must react to a conflict situation with force and aggression, thinking about his own self-respect and reputation among the inmate population through obedience to and compliance with the convict code.

Violence also becomes a means of reaffirming toughness and building self-preservation. In prison, inmates must stand their ground and constantly defend themselves and their property from attack. A violent demeanor is necessary for survival in prison as fighting is a way of communicating to other prisoners "not to mess with me." An inmate publicly bashing another inmate on the head with a pipe sends out the message that he won't take any abuse from anyone. It is a warning sign that he won't be pushed around and it will make other inmates think twice before they try to steal his property, give him some lip, take his place at the movies or attack him in the mess hall.

Inmates adopting the violent culture of the convict code will readily sell each other out. In a world where material possession is valued over self-respect and personal worth, convict life is based upon individuality, isolation and loneliness, undermining, as Irwin argues, any unifying effect the convict code may have once had (Irwin, 1970). Inmate interests are now expressed through the allegiance to a clique or gang, which becomes the basis of social solidarity. However, the presence of gangs, with their differential commitment to the convict code, has precluded the presence of factionalized interests which puts inmates at opposition with one another and creates division within the inmate population.

Gang members will readily rob, beat and attack those inmates who do not belong to a clique and who therefore have no basis of group protection. Status and power thus depends on gang membership and the ability to manipulate and control the racketeering activities within the inmate social system. In the past, the prison community was controlled by a few individuals, usually referred to as merchants and politicians (Sykes, 1958). These individuals were able to gain power through the formal organization of the prison by holding good jobs and using them to facilitate their illegal activities. However, in the modern prison, with the proliferation of drugs and gangs, the old con power structure dissipated and power and status are obtained through the informal organization of the inmate social system. Gang members, increasingly dominated by young offenders who do not care about being put in the hole for two weeks, have come to dominate and control the daily activities and routine operation of the prison community.

In the final analysis, the evidence shows that the social organization of the modern prison contributes to, encourages the development of and increases the amount and intensity of crime and violence. The patterns of interaction that emerge from the structure of prison organization are based on a complex social system with its own norms, values and methods of control. Throughout the history of corrections, this social system has ranged from the physical torture of the individual prisoner to the moral conviction of the criminal's lost soul. Today, harsh corporal punishment meted out by hostile guards, strictly enforced prison regulations and the dictatorial ruling of the prison administration is replaced by a system with no set policies, rules, regulations or criteria, a system which produces a climate of mental suffering, pressure and abuse that penetrates the heart and soul of every criminal in prison.

Anxiety, fear and tension permeate the life of the inmate. No longer can a prisoner do his time and know that when his time was up he can go out. He does not know if he will be dead or alive after five years, five days, five hours or even five minutes. There are no moments of peace in prison; never enjoy a meal too much, never get too involved when watching television, never close both eyes while taking a shower and never ever go into a deep sleep. Drugs, gangs, murder, disputes and violence permeate the life of the inmate in prison. Essentially, offenders are taken from an environment that encourages predatory criminal activity and placed in an environment which encourages these same activities and prisoners must go along with the negative in order to survive the prison experience. The only difference between criminal activity on the streets and criminal activity in prison is that in prison, where it is a closed environment, there is no place to run, nowhere to hide from your enemy. Insults, slights, disputes and other beefs cannot be ignored because you're constantly being watched by other inmates whose respect you must gain.

The prison experience thus has two effects on the individual prisoner. He can see it as merely an extension of the streets, a bitter reality of life as a hustler, something that is a risk of the trade, an evil that must be dealt with. While in prison, he will make the best out of his time to find ways to improve his enterprises on the streets. He will learn new tricks to be a more effective hustler. On the other hand, some convicts become so institutionalized, so used to the routines of prison life, that they cannot survive on the outside in the free world. They do not know how to make it in the real world. There are some inmates who get used to having decisions made for them and they have so internalized the convict code that their behavior cannot be altered to interact in free society (Clemmer, 1958). The portrayal of crime in the media and by politicians, along with the public outcry against crime and the emphasis on the harsh punishment of criminals has caused the prison administration to turn its back on the convict, who is regarded as a vicious and worthless criminal. The administration is therefore no longer concerned if an inmate saves some money to send to his family, if he gets an education or learns a trade or if he participates in activities that would facilitate his adjustment into society once released from prison. The dynamics of prison organization has left the administration content to control the prison population from mass riot and to prevent escapes, where the top priority is to clear the count. There is no emphasis on changing the behavior, attitude or outlook of inmates. While inside prison, inmates lack the motivation to acquire skills, clean up from using drugs and attempt to make for themselves a better life once released from prison. The structural forces of prison overcrowding, gang violence, drug trafficking and increase in youthful offenders have had a profound impact on the formal and informal organization of the prison institution. The dynamics of interaction within the prison have produced a population of violent, uncontrollable incarcerated individuals and a system of growing tolerance by staff for rule violation. The long term trend of such outcomes is the creation and maintenance of a class of criminals who are caught up in a vicious circle of rule violation and re-involvement in the criminal justice system, as violence, idleness and law breaking activities become the inevitable shadows of the prisoner behind bars. The prison experience thus has a profound effect on the behavior of the inmate once released from prison. Faced with long term deprivation, the inmate is surrounded for years by a community of violence, drugs and dangerous individuals, constantly exposed to ideas which express anger and hostility to free society. The inmate leaves prison haunted by memories and thoughts of his life behind bars and becomes more of a threat to society than when he first went in. The prison, while far from being a place which provides offenders with opportunities and incentives to refrain from illegal activities once released, actually places the inmate in an environment which makes him likely to become re-involved in criminal acts.

The inmate released from the hostile environment of prison must face the grim realities of life in free society (Ex-Offenders Task Force Meeting). He lacks the skills to get a decent job. He has no money to rent an apartment so he is forced to seek shelter elsewhere. Most often, the family of the ex-convict does not want anything to do with him, rejecting him for his life of crime and ashamed of his deviant acts. The ex-offender must face the humiliation and loss of self-dignity as he cannot escape the label of ex-con wherever he goes. Rejected by society, far away from the culture that once permeated his everyday life, the ex-offender has no where to turn but to the streets, to the old way of doing things, where thoughts of rehabilitation and a better life become a shattered dream against the bitter reality that going back to prison is only a heart beat away.

Of course not every prisoner returns to prison after being released. Deterrence does occur once in a while and an inmate will refrain from re-involvement in criminal activities. This occurs only when the inmate makes a conscious decision to change his life-style and it usually happens in spite of the system and not because of any moral convictions that took place while inside prison and especially not from any programs geared toward the transforming of offenders. Rehabilitation begins within the individual prisoner. As an ex-offender, he must overcome the stigma society has placed upon him and begin to make the right choices, develop a good attitude, hook up with the right people and get involved in community activities. Unfortunately, this occurs in a relative minority of ex-offenders and it usually happens to older inmates who have had enough of the hassles of being sent to the joint, again and again, in and out, day after day, year after year, and time after time (Ex-Offenders Task Force Meeting).

As the social organization of prisons have become increasingly marked by a culture of terror, violence, division and tension, prison officials are constantly in search for new and more effective ways of dealing with the growing inmate population. However, the new techniques of restoring order have the distinct quality of expanding and applying old formulas and failed ideas, creating a serious need for the re-evaluation of social policy. Accordingly, there are calls and pleas made by criminologists and social scientists for policies which cause a reduction in the criminal justice system and a build up of the social justice system through the reforming and transforming of crime producing social, political and economic institutions and policies (President, C.U.R.E. Organization). Efforts must be undertaken by lobbyists to make a change in legal statutes toward a de-criminalization of policies. Moreover, social policy must emphasize the urgent need for the presenting of solutions to the crime problem which calls for fewer rather than more prisons, as prisons are needed only for the truly dangerous, and not for all offenders. According to statistics, over 52.6% of **all** inmates admitted to State and Federal prisons are admitted for petty crimes while only 4.8% are admitted for very serious crimes. These data are based on the National Survey of Crime Severity. The "very serious crimes" category consists of crimes involving all of the following conditions: possession of a weapon, use of a weapon, injury to victim, possession of heroin or cocaine, child molestation and significant amount of money involved. The "petty crimes" category are crimes where none of the above conditions exit, and between the two extremes are the "moderate" and "serious" crime categories (see table 5).

Table 5. National Estimate of the Severity of Crimes
Committed by Persons Admitted to State and
Federal Prisons

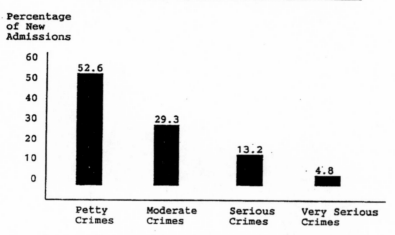

Percentage
of New
Admissions

Source: James Austin and John Irwin, Who Goes to
Prison?, San Francisco: National Council on
Crime and Delinquency, 1991 in "Policing the
Ghetto Underclass: the Politics of Law and
Law Enforcement," by William J. Chambliss,
Social Problems, Vol. 41, No. 2, May 1994.

Thus, society has a distorted reality of the individual offender. This is partially due to the representation of crime statistics in official reports which are subject to political manipulation, bias and discretionary police practices (Reiman, 1990; Chambliss, 1994). Social policy must reverse the image of inmates in prison as being mostly murderers, rapists, serial killers and social menaces, to a clear depiction of the humanity of the inmate. Criminal justice policy must reverse the trends of mandatory minimums, longer sentences and harsher penalties which have resulted in an unprecedented growth in the prison population. This is highly problematic in light of the fact that the crime rate has actually been stable for the past twenty years, while criminal justice policy calling for stricter punishments has been built up. Moreover, the evolution of penology is not accompanied by a subsequent reduction in criminal behavior. Victimization surveys indicate that the number of victimizations for all crimes has been relatively stable from 1973 to 1992, with relatively minor fluctuations (see table 6).

Table 6. Victimization Trends: 1973–1992

Number of
Victimizations

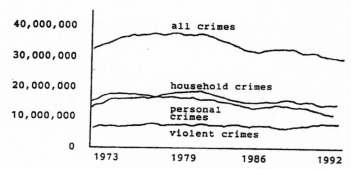

Source: Lucy N. Friedman, "Adopting the
Health Care Model to Prevent
Victimization", National Institute of
Justice Journal, November 1994, U.S.
Department of Justice, Office of
Justice Programs, National Institute
of Justice

However, the social policy implications outlined above must be understood within the context of the larger social structures and the various power struggles existing between interest groups competing for social change. Traditionally, historians, politicians, reformers and criminologists have viewed variations in incarceration rates, sentence lengths and physical punishment as occurring in response to the actual amount of crime in society. Thus, as crime rates rise, the agents in the criminal justice system tend to become more punitive as a way to deter criminals and potential criminals and thus curb the criminal trend. However, it is not sufficient to understand the structure and ideology of punishment as mere remedial reaction to the threat of crime. Correctional policies, practices and procedures ultimately affecting and shaping prison organization are also a product of power elites motivated by political and economic demands and interests. Irwin notes that "the criminal justice system is at least partially involved...in maintaining unfair social, political, and economic relationships" (Irwin, 1980, p. 230). The arrangement of the prison as presently organized and operated serves the private interests of certain segments of society, which far outweighs any efforts to reform, rearrange, reduce or eliminate the present system of corrections (Reasons, 1974). Thus, the system of corrections is maintained and perpetuated by those power forces in society who support the law and whose interests are served by the law and its justice system. It is important to note that these private sectional interests are not the only reason for the existence of prisons. For, society in general would agree to the isolation of those members who represent a threat to its well being. However, this social interest must be weighed against the economic and political demands of power elites. Most obviously served by the organization of prisons are prison personnel. Prisons employ thousands of individuals each year as prison guards, counselors, case workers, unit managers, probation officers and parole board officers (Haas and Alpert, 1991; Christie, 1993). Prisons area place where marginal professionals are employed; often, these individuals have minimal degrees which would not qualify them to practice in other more professional contexts. Prison guards in particular have relatively low educational attainment and it is especially difficult for them to find jobs in the labor market. Prisons, then, serve to "absorb" individuals from the labor market who might otherwise have difficulty finding employment.

Further opportunities and jobs are created for contractors who build prison facilities and those industries who supply goods to prisons. The explosion of new commitments to prison and the subsequent overcrowding of already existing facilities has turned the construction and operation of correctional facilities into a multi- billion dollar industry for private corporations (Anderson, 1991). Stricter sentencing measures, increased convictions and longer sentences, combined with increases in annual state and federal spending for prisons have all worked together to maintain an interest among the powerful private sector to keep and even to expand the correctional system as presently organized and operated.

Prisons are also very important to the field of medical research, as inmates are a vital source of subjects for various groups requiring human subjects for testing (Christie, 1993). The population of captives is a rich source of data for medical, psychological and sociological testing. Prisoners are used to test new products, especially drugs, for effectiveness and possible toxicity, explore new psychotherapy techniques and conduct various experiments procedures and analyses. But inmates in these experiments are not at all motivated by humanitarian reasons, but the hope of special treatment, favor or an early parole in exchange for their cooperation. Thus, the prison system provides a large pool of apparently willing and inexpensive experimental subjects whose availability and vulnerability increase the profits of drug companies, medical doctors, scientists and other interest groups seeking to make a profit.

Prisons also serve the interest of state and private industry by providing a form of slave labor (Christie, 1993). Prisoners are the prime producers of products for the state such as license plates, furniture for government offices, traffic signs and road signals, and agricultural goods. Inmates are also used inside the facility to do landscaping, cut grass and rebuild damaged structures. Wages for such labor are so extremely low that the labor provided by inmates could be and rightly should be called slave labor. The inmate on an average work assignment earns 12 cents an hour. If the penitentiary did not exist, the state would be forced to turn to the open market and hire labor at competitive wages, rather than prison labor. This would explain why attempts to institute minimum wage laws in prison are regarded as a threat by state officials and prison administrators (Liska, 1992; Christie, 1993).

Private enterprise is also served by prison labor, as prisoners are rented out to private businesses, industries and contractors, at very low cost (Reasons, 1977; Christie, 1993). Private industry is also served in another way by the low wage pool of ex-convicts produced by the prison system. A common condition of parole is that an inmate must have a job waiting for him when he leaves the institution. The prospective employer knows that the inmate has few options and will take very low wages. Moreover, the stigma of being an ex-convict continues to make job security tenuous for them, resulting in a reluctance to ask for higher wages and better working conditions. Illegal enterprises also flourish from the goods supplied to prisons. Corrupt prison officials can arrange with private corporations such as restaurants, contractors, computer parts sales and other companies, to provide them with goods at rates lower than market value, in return for a cut of the profits. These goods are stolen from the prison supply and often leave prisoners with a severe shortage of necessary products. This is a risky game that is played be a relative minority of staff and cannot continue to flourish without the help of inmate accomplices who must also share in the profits and risks incurred.

Finally, the prison system serves to legitimize the State's efforts at crime control (Chambliss and Seidman, 1971; Reiman, 1990; Liska, 1992). It allows the State to manipulate the public into believing that the crime problem is being solved efficiently and effectively, as more and more offenders are being placed behind bars. The legitimizing function of prisons is also seen as beneficial to those in positions of power. Conflict theorist Jeffery Reiman argues that the criminal justice system is designed to produce a distorted image of the crime problem in American society (Reiman, 1990). Arrest records, court decisions and sentencing convictions all have the effect of identifying those acts which are dangerous to society as primarily the work of the poor, urban black youth population. However, this represents a distorted image of the real crime problem in society as Reiman notes that "we have a greater chance of being killed or disabled by occupational injury or disease, unnecessary surgery, or by shoddy emergency medical services than by aggravated assault or even homicide" (Reiman, 1990). Yet, the perpetrators of these crimes rarely become part of the criminal population as reflected in arrest records and prison statistics. While a big corporate executive committing millions of dollars worth of fraud can get off, a man who steals a loaf of bread goes to jail. Thus, when we look into our prisons, the image we have of who poses a threat to our well-being are the poor, minority population, maintaining the explicit ideology that we need to lock up more of these "dangerous" members of society.

Criminal justice policies calling for longer sentences, stricter penalties and more prisons are a direct reaction to the public outcry against the media portrayal of the growing crime problem. Ironically, society's reaction to crime and sentiments towards criminals is a direct result of criminal justice policies and practices which shape the public's conception of who and what is dangerous, giving the impression that the harms it is fighting are the **real** threats to society. Thus, even when people perceive that the criminal justice system is far from being perfect, they generally go in the direction of demanding more of the same: more police, harsher penalties, getting tough on crime, building more prisons and putting more ghetto youth behind bars (Reiman, 1990).

The ideology of punishment and corrections, by focusing on the individual acts of the "dangerous" classes, has the outcome of diverting the attention away from the social and economic inequalities manifested in our social and political institutions that have direct benefit for those in power. Reiman concludes that "when the system holds an individual responsible for a crime, it implicitly conveys the message that the social conditions in which the crime occurred are not responsible for the crime, that they are not so unjust as to make a violent response to them excusable" (Reiman, 1990).

The picture painted by our present system of corrections, the faces we see and even imagine in our American prisons, has the effect of reaffirming and legitimating current power structures within society. By relaying the message that the threat to middle class Americans comes from the poverty stricken end of the economic ladder, it deflects the fear and unrest of the middle-class, who might otherwise turn against the unfair and oppressive practices of the wealthy upper class.

My analysis of our prison system paints a very grim reality. The wheels of injustice continue to spin as the weak voice of reform is silenced by the shouts of the powerful who desire to maintain the status quo. A lawyer once said that "corrections' worst nightmare is they would succeed in rehabilitating criminals...then they would have to shut down" (Mitchell, 1994). These words point to the urgent need for the radical revision of our system of corrections. It also highlights the problem that revisionists must face as they, representing the weakest and least desirable members of society, the criminals, the victims of the system, are up against the most powerful segments of society who have a vested interest in keeping the system as it is.

This study raises some very important issues. Prison policy and legislation must not be perceived as merely remedial reactions to the threat of crime. Society cannot adhere to the notion that our prisons are designed to meet our needs for protection from dangerous criminals and that changes in penal practices represent ideal responses to the demands of law enforcement and criminal justice. The public must look beyond the surface claims of prison policies into their ideological roots and logical origins. Policy makers cannot claim to be adequately addressing the issue of crime if our criminal justice policies and practices produce results which are the direct opposite of what they are supposed to achieve. Penal policies must correspond directly to the changing demands and needs of law enforcement, courts, prison administration and prisoners.

It is time to make clear an issue that is often misunderstood, distorted, manipulated and misrepresented by politicians, in popular literature and in the media. No longer can there be support for the continued use and expansion of the system of corrections as presently organized if its various characteristics, practices and procedures do not adequately address the continuing problem of crime in society. However, the connection made in this research about the relationship between correctional policy and the political and economic interests of power elites are highly general. In order to challenge prison policies today, the validity of these statements must be tested by examining in detail the political battles that were fought over prison legislation and policy changes in state legislatures, at corporate meetings, in church sermons, behind the doors of wardens' offices, in the reformer's mind and in the prisoner's dormitory.

The structure and goals of my research did not allow for the completion of this enormous endeavor and I therefore leave this task to future inquiry into penological study. The issues raised and claims made by this research must be qualified with the limitation that prisons do not uniformly correspond to the various descriptions stemming from the study of Lorton Central Prison. The diversity of institutions, the use of specialized treatment facilities and the unique qualities of each inmate population have produced differences between prisons. However, the dynamics of organization at Central prison and the various social relations that develop are relevant to the vast majority of higher security prisons across the United States. Moreover, the structure of social organization is influenced by emerging economic and political trends which raise various issues and ideologies, providing prisons and prisoners with a common background to share the same experiences of a specific historical time period. Each time period has its own unique forces of social change and evolution. It is hoped that this research has contributed to the positive movement of society in the direction of achieving a greater knowledge and understanding of the social organization of the modern prison.

Bibliography

Adamson, Christopher. (1984). "Toward a Marxian Penology: Captive Criminal Populations as Economic Threats and Resources," Social Problems, vol. 31, pp. 435-458.

.Anderson, George. (1991) . "Prisons and Money," America, vol. 164, pp. 516 - 519.

Bales, William, and Linda Dees. (1992) . "Mandatory Minimum Sentencing in Florida: Past Trends and Future Implications," Crime and Delinquency vol. 38, pp. 309-329.

Beccaria, Cesare. (1963) . On Crimes and Punishments. N.Y.: Bobbs-Merrill Co., Inc.

Beck, Allen, et al. (1993) . "Survey of State Prison Inmates: 1991, " U. S. Department of Justice, Office of Justice Programs, Bureau of Justice Statistics, Washington, D.C.

Bowker, Lee H. (1980) . Prison Victimization. New York Elsevier.

Braswell, Michael, et al. (1985) . Prison Violence in America. Cincinnati, Ohio: Anderson Pub. Co.

Carroll, Leo. (1974) . Hacks, Blacks, and Cons: Race Relations in a Maximum Security Prison. Illinois: Waveland Press.

Chambliss, William J., and Robert Seidman. (1971) . Law, Order and Power. Reading, Mass.: Addison-Wesley Pub. Co .

Chambliss, William J. (1973) . Sociological Readings in the Conflict Perspective. Reading, Mass.: Addison-Wesley Pub. Co.
_____(1994) "Policing the Ghetto Underclass: The Politics of Law and Law Enforcement," Social Problems, (May), Vol. 41, No. 2, pp. 177-194.

Christie, Nils. (1993) . Crime Control as Industry: Towards Gulgags, Western Style? London: N.Y.: Routledge.

Clemmer, Donald. (1958) . The Prison Community. NY: Rinehart and Company, Inc.

Cohen, R.L. (1991) . Prisoners in 1990. Washington, D.C. Department of Justice, Bureau of Justice Statistics.

Colvin, Mark. (1992) . The Penitentiary in Crisis: Accommodation to Riot in New Mexico. NY: State University of New York Press.

Cressey, Donald R. (1961). The Prison: Studies in Institutional Organization and

Chance. NY: Holt, Rinehart, and Winston, Inc.

Crouch, Ben M. (1991) . "Guard Work in Transition," Chapter 10 in Haas and Alpert. (1991). Dilemmas of Corrections. Illinois: Waveland Press, Inc.

Crouch, Ben and James W. Marquart. (1980) . "On Becoming a Prison Guard," in B. Crouch. (1980) . The Keepers: Prison Guards and Contemporary Corrections. Illinois: Charles C. Thomas Publishers.

Davidson, Theodore. (1983) . Chicano Prisoners: The Key to San Quentin. Illinois: Waveland Press.

DiIulio, John J. (1987) . Governing Prisons: A Comparative Study of Correctional Management. New York: Free Press.

Domhoff, G. W. (1990). The Power Elite and the State: How Policy is Made in America. New York: Walter De Gruyter, Inc.

Eitzen, Stanley D. (1985) . Criminology. New York: John Wiley and Sons.

Feeley, Malcolm, and Jonathan Simon. (1992). "The New Penology: Notes on the Emerging Strategy of Corrections and its Implications," Criminology, vol. 30, pp. 449-474.

Fleisher, Mark S. (1989) . Warehousing Violence. California: Sage Publications.

Fong, Robert S. and Salvador Buentello. (1991). "The Detection of Prison Gang Development: An Empirical Assessment," Federal Probation, vol. 55, (March), pp. 66-69.

Friedman, Lucy N. (1994). "Adopting the Health Care Model to Prevent Victimization," National Institute of Justice Journal, U.S. Department of Justice, Office of Justice Programs, National Institute of Justice, Washington, D.C.

Garrity, Donald L. (1961) . "The Prison as a Rehabilitation Agency," Chapter 6 in Cressey, Donald R. (1961). The Prison Studies in Institutional Organization and Chance. N.Y.:Holt, Rinehart and Winston, IncGilliard, Darrell, et al. (1993). "Prisoners in 1993," U.S. Department of Justice, Office of Justice Programs, Bureau of Justice Statistics, Washington, D.C.

Goffman, Irving. (1961) . Asylums. NY: Anchor Books, Doubleday and Company, Inc.

Haas, Kenneth C., and Geoffrey P. Alpert. (1991) . The Dilemmas of Corrections. Illinois: Waveland Press, Inc.

Hazelrigg, Lawrence E. (1969) . Prison Within Society: a Reader in Penology. Garden City, N.Y.: Doubleday.

Irwin, John. (1970). The Felon. NJ: Prentice-Hall, Inc.

_____(1980) . Prisons in Turmoil. Boston, Toronto Little, Brown and Company.

obs, James B. (1974). "Participant Observation in Prison," Urban Life and Culture Vol. 3, No. 2 (July) 221 - 240.
_____(1977) . Stateville: The Penitentiary in Mass Society. Chicago: University of Chicago Press.
_____(1983) . New Perspectives on Prisons and Imprisonment. Ithaca: Cornell University Press.

oby, Joseph E. (1979) . Classics of Criminology. Illinois: Waveland Press, Inc.

ik, Nancy C. (1985) . "Individual and Organizational Determinants of Correctional Officer Attitudes Toward Inmates," Criminology, vol. 23, (April), p. 523-539.

linich, David B. (1980) . The Inmate Economy. Massachusetts: Lexington Books

ka, Allen. (1992) . Social Threat and Social Control. Albany: State University of New York Press.

ckwood, Daniel. (1980) . Prison Sexual Violence. New York: Elsevier North Holland.

fland, John and Lyn H. Lofland. (1984). Analyzing Social Settings: Guide to Qualitative Observation and Analysis. California: Wadsworth Pub. Co.

mbard, Lucien X. (1981) . Guards Imprisoned: Correctional Officers at Work. New York: Elsevier.

read, Joseph and Lawrence Hazelrigg. (1972) . Class, Conflict, and Mobility: Theories and Studies of Class Structure. San Francisco: Chandler Pub. Co.

ris, Ronald W. (1988) . Social Problems. Chicago: Dorsey Press.

rquart, James W. and Julian B. Roebuck. (1985) . "Prison Guards and Snitches: Deviance Within a Total Institution," The British Journal of Sociology, (July), p. 217-233.

rquart, James W. (1986). "Prison Guards and the Use of Physical Coercion as a Mechanism of Prisoner Control, Criminology, vol. 24, (May), p. 346-366.

rx, Karl. (1904). Contribution to a Critique of Political Economy. N.Y.: Modern Library

rx, Karl and Friedrich Engels. (1968). The German Ideology. Moscow: Progress Publishers.

yhew, Leon H. (1982) . Talcott Parsons: On Institutions and Social Evolution.

Chicago: The University of Chicago Press.

Miles, Matthew B. and A.M. Huberman. (1994). Qualitative Data Analysis: An Expanded Sourcebook. Thousand Oaks: Sage Publications.

Mitchell, Thomas. (1994). Interview with Aida Yassa, 31 May 1994, Washington, D.C.

Pontell, Henry N., and Wayne N. Welsh. (1994) . "Incarceration as a Deviant Form of Social Control: Jail Overcrowding in California," Crime and Delinquency. vol. 40, p . 18-36.

Pray, Roger T. (1987) . "How Did Our Prisons Get That Way?" American Heritage. Vol. 38, (July), pp. 38-52.

Reiman, Jeffrey. (1990). The Rich Get Richer and the Poor Get Prison. NY: Macmillan Pub. Co.

Reasons, Charles. (1974) . "Tear Down the Walls? Some Functions of Prisons," The Ideology of Social Problems.

Rusche, Georg, and Otto Krichheimer. (1939). Punishment and Social Structure. Albany: State University of New York Press.

Saltzburg, Stephen A. (1993). Oral History Interview with Aida Yassa, 25 May 1993, Washington, D.C.

Sampson, Robert and John Laub. (1993). Crime in the Making. Mass.: Harvard University Press

Scacco, Anthony M. (1975). Race in Prison. Springfield, Ill.: C.C. Thomas.

Spierenburg, Peter. (1987). "From Amsterdam to Auburn: An Explanation for the Rise of the Prison in Nineteenth Century America," Journal of Social History. vol. 20.

Sykes, Gresham M. (1958). The Society of captives. NJ: Princeton University Press.

Tonry, Michael. (1993). "The Failure of U.S. Sentencing Commissions' Guidelines," Crime and Delinquency. vol. 39, pp. 131-149.

Trestar, Harold. (1981). Supervision of the Offender. New Jersey: Prentice Hall.

Tucker, Robert C. (1978). The Marx-Engels Reader. NY: W.W. Norton and Company.

United States Congress. (1984). U.S. Code of Congressional and Administrative News. G.P.O., Washington, D.C.

155

Van Maanen, John, et al. (1982). <u>Varieties of Qualitative Research.</u> CA: Sage
    Publications.

Vold, George. (1958). <u>Theoretical Criminology.</u> NY: Oxford University Press.

Name Index

Subject Index

administration, 4, 27, 29, 32, 47

assault, 148

Auburn System, 40-41

capital punishment, 37-38

Central Prison, 30-33, 45-51

Conflict Theory, 9-16

contraband, 4, 28, 44, 46, 47, 65-72, 74, 76, 79, 80, 86, 90, 100

corporal punishment, 38-40

correctional officer, 31-34, 55, 69, 89-92, 97, 98, 114-119

criminogenic, 24

custody, 57

dehumanization, 121

determinate sentencing, 2, 43-44

drugs, 4, 28-32, 73-85, 97, 99, 103, 105-109, 121, 124, 125, 132, 137-139

Enlightenment, 38

fag, 19, 87

food services, 52, 64-67

freak, 101-109

gangs, 3, 27, 28, 44, 80-82, 124-130, 135-137

health care, 53, 54, 58

homosexuality, 31-32, 65, 68, 88, 135

intake, 58-59

indeterminate sentencing, 41-43

law suits, 35, 95

loner, 86-87

mandatory minimums, 2, 29, 143

major dealer, 83

merchant, 19, 26, 28, 80, 137

Muslims, 53, 81, 129

overcrowding, 4, 8, 29, 31, 32, 40-43, 125, 132, 138, 145-146

Pennsylvania System, 39-40

politician, 26-29

prisonization, 23-24

programming, 132

protective custody, 85, 112

psychologists, 119

punishment, 3, 9, 12, 39

punk, 19, 67, 85-86

Pyrric Defeat Theory, 15

race, 44

racketeering, 28, 31, 71-73, 80, 105

rape, 29, 38, 39, 44, 68, 118, 131

reform, 13, 35, 38-43, 140, 145, 149

rehabilitation, 3, 24, 28, 32, 40, 43, 53, 57, 79, 97, 98, 121, 130-134, 139-140

riots, 91, 95, 138

screw ups, 98-100

security, 57

Sentencing Guidelines, 2-3

159

CRIMINOLOGY STUDIES